People don't grow by being measured

recollections and reflections of a dyslexic grandmother

Brenda Crowe

People don't grow by being measured

recollections and reflections of a dyslexic grandmother

Matador
9 De Montfort Mews
Leicester LE1 7FW, UK
Tel: (+44) 116 255 9311 / 9312
Email: books@troubador.co.uk
Web: www.troubador.co.uk/matador

ISBN 978-1906510-299 PPB
ISBN: 978-1848760-189 HB

A Cataloguing-in-Publication (CIP) catalogue record for this book is available from the British Library.

Typeset in 12pt Bembo by Troubador Publishing Ltd, Leicester, UK
Printed in the UK by MPG Biddles, Kings Lynn, Norfolk

Matador is an imprint of Troubador Publishing Ltd

To my mother

CONTENTS

Foreword

I first met Brenda Crowe in 1984 when we were involved in a series of programmes for Thames TV called " Understanding Toddlers." Brenda's wisdom and understanding and her total concentration when listening struck me immediately. She gave me a vision of a child's world, of play and of learning, of what children feel in relation to adults, which opened my eyes to completely new ways of thinking. As she described her own rural childhood and how she had played, it struck many chords with my own upbringing in a remote Cumbrian valley. I too, like her, had learned many things from play, that "self-chosen activity, undertaken for its own sake."

This highly individual book is a loving portrayal of a dyslexic child growing up in a world that readers over 55 will instantly recognise. Brenda's memory for the details, colour and sounds of life in rural East Anglia over eighty years ago is remarkable.

But then she did not know she was dyslexic. She had a happy and untroubled childhood, and it was only when she went to school that she learned to think that there was something "wrong" with her, that she was of low to average intelligence and hopeless at anything mechanical. She was also unable to read well enough to enjoy a book.

But at the age of eighty, having decided to be tested for dyslexia, she found she was "highly intelligent" and had "exceptional strengths." This was no surprise to those of us who knew her, but gave Brenda a feeling of euphoria. What had changed of course was her perception of herself.

This fascinating book is a result of that eye-opener. And in it Brenda reflects on her own pattern of learning, on her vivid sensory memories and joy in colour, and emphasises how she "was allowed to develop in my own time and way before (starting) school."

Brenda also learned, at first hand, many things about the contribution of family life to child development, when she travelled the country in the early 60s staying in the homes of members of the Pre-school Playgroups Association of which she was a pioneer.

From her own experience she draws out illuminating lessons on child-rearing, about the importance of a child's own perception of their achievements, about timing, about not growing by being measured, and about all the things we learn by doing them for ourselves.

This is a book full of remarkable insights and the wisdom of someone who has continued in life-long learning with an open mind and a great sense of humour.

It's about the things I wish all children could have: firm and loving support from their family, imbuing them with the confidence to find things out for themselves, to be allowed to grow at their own speed and to feel normal when approaching any problem "in their own way."

Anna Ford

August 2007

CHAPTER 1

In at the deep end

How I discovered I was dyslexic

When I was 80 I read a magazine article on dyslexia that rang bells for me – I had always known that I couldn't spell, and that I never wanted to read books, but was there more to it than that?

I have loved my life, and didn't mind in the least that I wasn't cut out for an academic career. Yet, in spite of not wanting it there was always the background feeling of inferiority that said, "Just as well you didn't want it, because you simply haven't got what it takes to get A-levels and go to a university."

The bells in my head were so insistent that they could no longer be ignored, so I contacted the address at the end of the article and arranged to be officially tested.

Some of the tests I could do easily; with others, I started well but reached cut-out point very quickly and abruptly; yet others I started with cautious optimism, but I reached a stage where I felt it beginning to slip away, and although I made a huge effort to hold on to what I had whilst reaching out to grasp the next bit, everything went beyond recall.

At the end of the test, which took two hours, we chatted for a bit, and then the examiner asked, "How have you regarded yourself all these years?" I said I knew exactly: I was of low to average intelligence, poor at spelling, unable to read well enough to enjoy a book, hopeless at maths beyond simple addition and subtraction, and even worse at science or anything mechanical. On the other hand I was capable, cope-able, practical, had sound common sense, was good with my hands and creative in thought and action, adding, "I can live with all this very happily."

He weighed this up for a bit, and said, "Then you would be genuinely surprised to know that you are intelligent, in fact highly intelligent?" I said I would be totally amazed, and he added, "Even now you could go to university and get a degree in anything you liked."

The test showed conclusively that I *am* dyslexic, and pin-pointed those areas where my difficulties lay and – surprise, surprise! – those areas where I had exceptional strengths. The aftermath was extraordinary. I went about for the next three days in a state of euphoria, saying to myself, "I'm intelligent, I'm *highly* intelligent!" I couldn't get over the idea.

The relief was overwhelming. I felt as though I had had a cataract operation on my brain – suddenly light and colour flooded in, transforming everything. So much that had been a mystery was explained, and instead of a background of inadequacy I felt elated and excited. The impact was illogical for nothing had changed – except my perception of myself.

That was it! It wasn't just 'me'; there had been a real problem there all the time.

But was my dyslexia a 'problem'? Had there really been something 'wrong' with me all that time? I couldn't believe it, but in the light of my work with distressed or 'opted-out' dyslexics years later, I felt the need to go back over my recollections with the eyes of experience.

I needed to try to discover whether there were signs that I might have been dyslexic before school and, if so, what those signs were. If not, then was there something in my early and wonderfully happy childhood that strengthened me to rise above, or work around, this 'handicap' later? Or was it a blockage, or a series of blockages and gaps, that became the source of so much of my joy as I learned to circumnavigate them?

I think it could have been a tragedy if I had had so much 'help' to conform to what I was never intended to be, that it deflected me from the tides and currents that are finally bringing me to where I feel I was intended to be.

Having said that, I do indeed know that although I have been such a happy and fulfilled dyslexic, this same condition (in all its degrees and manifestations) has blighted too many lives for it not to be the focus of teachers' and parents' attention – and I would like to contribute to their learning if I can.

Spreading the word

After my initial joy at discovering I was dyslexic, I was happy for anyone to know about it – it was clearly helpful to those who suddenly sensed the possibility of feeling up-beat about it, instead of down-cast by being 'different'.

But then I became disenchanted at being pigeon-holed. It came back to me that people were very 'surprised'. Why were their associations with the word so uniformly negative?

Some said that I "wasn't," because although my spelling was weak it was no worse than that of many others.

Many said, with disbelief and not a little irritation, "Of *course* you must have known you were intelligent." But I didn't. The qualities and strengths of dyslexics often don't show up in school tests and exams – and even if they did, they wouldn't add up to 'intelligence' in the context of academic measurements.

Others said, "Of *course* you can learn from books. You can read aloud perfectly well; you just have to try harder." But I can't bridge the gap between what I read and what the writers are trying to tell me, especially if the words form no pictures in my mind.

Most frequently of all I am told, "A word processor would correct your spelling and speed things up," and I am back to square one, trying to explain about the gaps that defeat me. My mind, eye, hand, biro and paper have to be in direct contact with each other – I *can't* look at a screen and change a sentence without writing it down.

This time round, my confidence is no longer threatened. People are free to think and say what they like, and I am grateful to those who make a serious attempt to understand, but only I know what goes on – or doesn't, because it can't – inside my head. I must stand my ground now.

Because I know how it is for me, I have always been able to communicate with those who have similar difficulties, whatever their age. I can talk to them face to face, or talk on paper (the only way I can write), but always in word pictures backed up by for-instances.

Now that I know I am dyslexic, and can describe my difficulties more clearly, people jump in saying, "I know exactly! That's just the way it is for me!" And I feel the need to take this further, before it is too late.

I have reached the age of wanting to simplify my home and my life, and have slowly gone through every drawer, cupboard and shelf, including the garage and the garden shed, to see what I use and still enjoy, and what is surplus to my present needs. It has been a nostalgic and fascinating process, filled with memories, and I can't bring myself to throw anything away – I need to find 'good homes' for everything. By this same token, I also want to pass on as much of my learning as may be relevant, in the hope that there may insights here which could also find 'good homes' and continue to be useful.

Now comes the moment when I have to decide how, and indeed if, I can find 'good homes' for these recollections and reflections.

At first I thought it was just for me wanting to review my happy childhood again to see if I could spot any signs that I was – or might possibly become – dyslexic once formal education began.

But a straightforward autobiography isn't the answer – it might

6

give nostalgic pleasure to some of those over 60, it might even be useful in schools as part of a history project on 'how it used to be'. But that would miss the point of what I really want to do.

At this point, I decided to write for dyslexics and their parents, to explain that we can be very valuable in our own right – but only if teachers and parents can come to understand *how we learn* and *to what end*. But, as with any book, this is for anyone, whoever and whatever they are, who finds that it speaks to them.

When I began to think along these lines and discuss it with others, they sensibly said, "But if they can't read and don't go into libraries and bookshops, how are they going to know what you have written?"

Good question. The only answer seemed to be, "By chance."

Then I remembered a letter written to me by a playgroup mother shortly after 'Living with a Toddler' had been published. She said, "I thought you would like to know that my husband didn't come to bed until three o'clock this morning. I said, 'What have you been doing?' And he said, 'Reading that book you left on the table,' and I said, 'But you don't read!' and he replied, 'I know, but that isn't a proper book, is it? I can hear her talking to me.'."

I have met this reaction many times since and I too can read if I hear somebody telling me something I want to know. We should never assume people can't do something, just because they *think* they can't. Under certain circumstances, they sometimes can.

I should be sorry if the fact that I hardly ever read was interpreted as meaning I wasn't interested in other people's thoughts and ideas. I am, profoundly. If people will share their thinking with me, I respond like a desert to a down-pour. And *then* I can learn.

For a great many of my kind of dyslexic, it isn't the ideas we don't understand, but the form of words (too many concepts; too few pictures) that obscures the meaning.

So I decided first to re-think the timeless nature of play itself, which is an area where I feel at home, having done it, and tried to promote it, all my life.

Just what is it that I want to pass on?

I want to try to reveal childhood as the wondrous state and stage of our lives that it truly is – or could be if only children were given more time, and adults were more in tune with children's *simple* needs, and less anxious about giving them 'a good start' in other directions.

Central to childhood is spontaneous play, so I want to write about that, but I don't want to create a recipe book of play activities, for that concept of play – toys, games, activities and 'educational play' – is almost completely self-defeating.

My sister Pauline and I were always very close and we did a lot of thinking, comparing notes, and putting two and two together when our mother was in her eighties. We were in complete agreement that we wouldn't have changed a thing about our home-based childhood. (School was another matter.)

Our childhood was deeply rooted in the reality of every day life, just because it was there to be lived and enjoyed for its own sake – not as a getting-ready for anything else. Everything sprang naturally from what we were doing, and what we were doing was whatever came to hand according to the needs of the day.

There was *time*, time to look and touch, time to watch and contemplate, time for repetition, time alone and time together, time to laugh and shout and time to be quiet, time to be slow – time, wonderful time, it stretched out forever, yet it could go in a flash. We made our way through it under our own steam; we weren't pulled or pushed, or deflected. (At least, that was how it felt at the time and how it appears in retrospect.)

There was no teaching-talk; we remembered talk only as between people (whatever their age or relationship) who had something to say, or explain, or ask.

There were amazing things to do that were all new at first, though the real art of doing each job became apparent with practice – whether it was making scones or mud pies; changing the bed linen or making and re-making our dolls' beds; sorting the laundry, or sorting Grandma's button box; shopping, or making a shop in the kitchen or the garden.

Where does the line lie between work and play? To children, there is no line – unless the adults they live with make it apparent that 'work' is a chore to be got through, without any kind of pleasure or satisfaction. Our attitude to all aspects of life is coloured by the adults who introduce us to it, on a daily basis, particularly in the pre-school years.

We were lucky to have parents who loved their jobs: father loved his hands-on farming, and Mother loved bringing up her family, with all the daily and seasonal jobs that that entailed, and we loved being a part of it all.

Because I feel sure that my dyslexia didn't manifest itself (at least to me) during the pre-school years, I want to write about our family life, which capitalised on all our natural strengths, and minimised so many of the later difficulties. I think I can only record the journey of my life as I remember it, using the clarity of my pictorial and sensory memories, in the hope that some of my memories may spark some of your own.

If they also throw light on the way in which children (not only dyslexics) learn, that will be a bonus. Family life before school is supremely important for *every* child – whatever the future may hold, whatever children's strengths or weaknesses compared with expectations based on what is perceived to be 'average' or 'normal'.

It doesn't matter whether you believe my memories or agree with my thoughts. What matters is that it stirs *your* memories – of your childhood, your parents, your home, in your own time and community.

The more you think about, share and compare (not measure) your memories, the more apparent it will be that there is no one pattern for a valuable family. We each have our starting-point and make our way from there with love and commitment.

As you re-discover and re-define your own family values, and how you learn best, sing it aloud from the house-tops; don't let what you know be undermined and lost in legislation at this crucial point in our history.

What is dyslexia?

I have been trying to find a definition of dyslexia that would be helpful to people like me. But I can't.

The irony is that although I can recognise that the definitions in books and articles are *about* me, they are not directly available *to* me. I can't understand them.

I can read them slowly, and with much going back to the beginning of the sentence. But at the end of it, I haven't understood. Why? I love words, and their meanings, and trying to find exactly the right word to express what I think, or feel, or need. I love talking and listening and thinking. I have no problem with any of that. So why can't I learn from print as easily as I can learn from people?

Let me give you an example of my difficulty (but if you know at once that reading the definition in the next paragraph is going to defeat you too, then skip it and join me further down the page).

The World Federation of Neurology defines dyslexia as, "a disorder manifested by difficulty in learning to read despite conventional instruction, adequate intelligence and socio-cultural opportunity. It is dependent upon fundamental cognitive disabilities which are frequently of constitutional origin."

I read this definition again and again, word by word. Then I tried to re-write it, in more familiar language, and it looked like this: "Dyslexia is a disorder that makes it difficult for people to learn to read – even though they are taught reading at school, and are reasonably intelligent, and have a helpful home background. It is due to difficulties that are there at birth."

This translation is not as accurate as the original, but at least it conveyed to me the following information:

- It is not my fault.
- It is not my parents' fault.
- It is not my teachers' fault
  (though some were more helpful than others).
- Something was different at birth.

From other sources I gathered that:

- It can't be cured – (though we can be greatly helped to overcome it).
- It won't go away – (but we can learn to welcome many aspects of it).
- It won't improve – (but our ability to live with it, and benefit from it, does).
- It can be present in people of high, low or average intelligence.
- It can be slight or severe.
- It may also affect mathematical ability in some people
  (definitely me).

Dyslexics are very definitely not second-class *people* – we can be first-class *people* but in a different sphere altogether.

Even if we are not very intelligent, we can still be first-class people.

Other snippets of information that I have gathered include the fact that, "Many dyslexics excel in the visual arts, music and the theatre."

At first I was amazed by the well-known names of those who were, I discovered, dyslexic – then I became even more interested in their comments on their dyslexia.

The genius Albert Einstein was sacked from two teaching jobs for terrible spelling, and once said, "If I can't picture it, I can't understand it."

Thomas Edison, inventor behind the light bulb, said, "I almost decided I must be a dunce."

The celebrated chef Marco Pierre White believes his dyslexia gave him, "a compulsion to dissect ideas and concepts."

Racing driver Jackie Stewart quite obviously had no problems making judgements at high speed, and he said of himself, "Because I have to concentrate so hard, I can't let anything distract me."

Winston Churchill was a dismal and unhappy failure at school, but was always fascinated by history and the strategy of war. At the outbreak of war in 1939 he said, "This is the hour for which I was born," and his leadership and visionary speeches inspired our nation to hold on when the odds against us seemed overwhelming.

Jude Kelly said, on Desert Island Discs, that she was very anti-social at school, truanted and was nearly in trouble with the police; then a headmaster said to her, "You're an existentialist; your creativity is out of kilter – why don't we find a way of using it? Would you like it if I started a drama group in the lunch hour? If you don't get out of where you are, you'll get trapped." She would, and he did, and having found her vocation she went on to found the York Community Theatre, then on to the National Theatre, and then on again.

Recently, there has been the young chef Jamie Oliver, who breezed into a classroom clutching an armful of huge leeks, saying, "Who knows what these are?" Almost no one did, but his enthusiasm and practicality swept them up and carried them with him – the enthusiasm has now spread to dinner ladies, parents and teachers. A confident dyslexic at last!

Other dyslexics might identify with some, or all, of these well-known dyslexics. It is Albert Einstein and Marco Pierre White who speak to me most clearly.

So what of us more ordinary people? We are stranded between those who shine like stars in the academic field, and those who also shine like stars in other spheres. We are mere glow-worms by comparison!

A great many of us are extremely happy glow-worms, especially out of school, so don't feel too sorry for us. But we don't want to be made to feel that we are *dim* as we struggle on – we need to feel happy and hopeful, we need to feel that you like and appreciate us as *people,* that you understand how hard we are trying, and how difficult we find this particular method of learning from books, blackboards, writing, tests and exams. We would even like to ask you to question whether this is the best way of teaching us.

I found a helpful description that said dyslexia was rather like walking along a path, and suddenly finding your way blocked by a huge boulder. There is no way over, or under, or round this obstacle as far as you can see – but quite often we can be helped, inch by inch, to work our way round by a slightly longer route.

The ability to read is tremendously helpful, but it shouldn't be assumed that once we are round this huge boulder we shall be all set to 'catch up', and continue on our way towards GCSEs, A levels and university. *Don't be too ambitious for us to learn too soon in your way, towards your goals. Our way of learning, towards our as yet unrecognised goals, may be rather different.*

The downside of dyslexia takes so many forms that we can't compare anybody to anybody else. For example, I can read. If we had time I could read any of the daily papers aloud to you from cover to cover. I should certainly come to personal and place names that I wouldn't even attempt to pronounce, but apart from that, no problem.

The snag is that I should retain almost nothing, unless there was a picture to illustrate the text. Sometimes I read, and re-read, an article and then look away and ask myself what I have read – and I don't know.

I go to the theatre, and am totally absorbed in the play, then the interval comes and I want to know about a particular actor – so I look again at the programme. The print is too small, the facts too condensed, and I can't retain any of it.

I used to go to art exhibitions at the Royal Academy in London – but the minute I tried to read the information sheet printed large, just inside each gallery, it was like a shutter coming down. The printed word deadened everything.

Yet writing is easy – why? I long ago stopped worrying about spelling, but as long as I write longhand, I can write what I think even as I think it.

Sometimes people's letters to me can be difficult to decipher and translate – unless I know them very well, and then I just look at the paper and 'listen' to them; I can hear their individual voices quite clearly.

Mental arithmetic defeats me. I can't work out 10% of a bill. People say, "Move the point one place to the left," and I do, which means that £37.18 becomes £3.718 – and I am lost because there shouldn't be three figures. What are they, pence? No, because then I should have £7 something, on top of my £3. This has now been solved for me, once and for all, by a friend – we were having a meal in the kitchen, and I was telling him about this problem. He spotted the nature of the difficulty at once. He got up and fetched a bill-sized piece of paper from the dresser on which he wrote £37.18 and handed it to me on a plate, saying, "Now, pick it up with your thumb over the last figure, before you move your point to the left. What do you see?" Answer, £3.71. Once it was visual there was no problem.

There is also, for me, an up-side of dyslexia. I am inadequate at reading print, but I can 'read' anything that is of consequence to *me*, and my way of life. I can read people and situations – no matter how complicated working and personal relationships may be in any given situation. I can see the main picture, and everyone's unique angle on that same picture.

I can't move points around in arithmetic, but I can often help people to widen their personal views of a given situation, by explaining what the view looks like from several other perspectives. I am by no means alone in this, and I am not claiming credit as a dyslexic, I am just saying that for *me* this is one of *my* joys.

Similarly, I can 'read' a great deal about a child at first glance: Well-braced knees, and feet plonked firmly on the ground, say to me, "I may be a bit apprehensive, but I'm standing my ground against all comers…"

Slack knees, flexed ankles, feet almost apologising for taking up any room on the earth say, "I'm too scared to move. Don't ask me to respond to anyone or anything yet – just move in slowly, take my hand, and talk very quietly."

Eyes darting warily say, "What's going on? Am I safe?"

A bold sweep of the room says, "Wow! What am I going to do first?"

Eyes filling with tears tell me to ask Mum to stay until he's settled.

If there's a dash for the nearest thing on wheels, my legs are longer, so I get there first, in time to say, "I'm sure William will let you have a go when he's finished, won't you William?" (William won't let you down; children can 'read' situations just as quickly as us, if not quicker.)

There are many non-dyslexic people who can also 'read' children like this, and a great many of them are untrained and lacking in self-esteem. Those who are dyslexic, having felt sub-standard at school, suddenly find this affinity for children brings them the same joy that it brings me.

Many of us read hands in the same way. Young or old, hands can twitch, clench, flex easily, grip firmly or pick up a single grain of spilt sugar with the very tips of the first finger and thumb, or cringe from messy play because the child is afraid of getting dirty, or because some sensitive finger tips hate touching anything slimy, or rough, or knobbly, or furry or feathery.

Above all, each child has his or her own 'feel' – and this isn't something that all adults can sense, even if they are trained.

I can't remember people's names, but my photographic memory means that within the space of time that it takes to see someone advancing in my direction, about to say, "You won't remember me, but…" I can say truthfully, "Oh! Yes I do – you had the tallest rubber tree in the world in your hall!" or, "I remember you perfectly well – you had a new caravan in the front garden that you were about to try out. How did the holiday go?" or "You had just redecorated your daughter's bedroom – and made new curtains, with a covered house brick to match, to prop her door open so that she could see the landing light."

I can recall our wonderful holidays on Greek islands, long before they had been discovered, in exactly the same detail. I can lie in bed and swim again with my husband from the Durrells' White House, across Kalami bay, to sit for a while on the hot rocks, then back again to the steps up from the sea, to the little vine-clad terrace. As we sat down, the grilled trout we had ordered before we set off was carried out of the kitchen. I can recapture the heat of the sun, the quality of the air, the smell of warm ripe figs on the bushes, the sound of buzzing wasps, and the chatter and clatter from the kitchen.

These vivid sensory memories give me untold joy, again and again. We didn't even possess a camera, and for me particularly my mental

17

photograph album is better than a traditional one. Looking through photographs is jerky, "and this is where we… and this is the man who… and this is the taverna…" But with my sensory memories the times and events just flow, and I am there again. It may not sound a very practical, let alone a money-making gift – but it is beyond price to me. I have no way of knowing whether or not there is a link with dyslexia.

I can carry colour accurately in my head, and have no need to take patterns about with me. Colour, too, is one of my joys, and always has been. I have never worn black, brown or grey because when I catch sight of it as I look down or stretch out an arm, I feel drained of joy instead of a flash of joy. My garden is an ever-changing wash of colour, with foliage and flowers every day of the year.

I vividly remember the joy of spontaneous – not strictly ballroom! – dancing with my husband. We danced at the drop of a hat – on the lino in the kitchen if a quick-step was irresistible; on a pavement in our stout walking shoes if we were on a Spring holiday in Spain and heard live music coming from a café. Sometimes we were spotted, fetched inside and given an empty floor to dance on, followed by applause, coffee, cake and brandy. We loved the spontaneous acceptance by the black-clad figures of the local people, enjoying their Sunday afternoon ritual. We had no formal language in common, but the language of music, dance, laughter and good fellowship is universal.

I am not the only person to have discovered these joys, but as a dyslexic they are in complete contrast to the struggling, downbeat frustration and boredom of much of my school life and are particularly valued.

On balance, do I regret that I am dyslexic? No, not for a single second. But I am profoundly grateful that I was allowed to develop in my own time and way before school, and that I never had to earn parental love by performing well once I was in the school system.

CHAPTER 2

Introduction to the world through my family

My background

My parents were married in 1918, a union that suited both of them to perfection for over sixty years, but which caused shock waves in both families. Mother was deemed to have married beneath her, and Father was thought to be asking for trouble by marrying a la-di-dah girl who looked more suited to the top of a chocolate box than a farmhouse and muddy yard.

How wrong they all were!

Mother had hated school, and working in her Father's office during the war, and the snobbery and hypocrisy of their social circle, and above all the upsets and lack of understanding within her family. She loved the country and animals, and the only thing in the world she wanted to do was to marry a farmer and to live in the country and bring up a family.

Father was one of the working sons of a working farmer, who had fallen in love with the daughter of a rather grand local farmer. The girl's formidable mother had pronounced him not good enough and sent him packing.

So, there they were one evening, two strangers attending a Christmas dance in the Ilford Town Hall, Father still feeling somewhat flat and joyless, and Mother feeling as any girl would whose father always insisted, "You don't want a new dress, dear; just wash your hands and face and put on a smile."

Father gave her one look and said to his brother, "That's the girl I am going to marry," and asked her to dance. Mother accepted, and said later, "I knew at once; it just felt so completely right."

Neither of them had any doubts, nor did their wise and loving parents, but the assorted brothers, sisters and relatives were less perceptive. There wasn't much to choose between the snobs of one family and the inverted snobs of the other. Father was serenely untroubled, having got his 'fairy off the top of the Christmas tree', but Mother was deeply hurt for both of them.

Within a matter of weeks Father had asked permission of her family, and proposed. Mother had accepted, and Father had said, "The wedding will have to be after seed-time in March, or after the harvest in September. Which would you like?" Bearing in mind that a large wedding was inevitable, Mother chose September.

The long-term plan was for them to move into the farmhouse after the death of both Father's parents, but meanwhile to live within a few miles of the farm and commute daily. Before the war a small estate of assorted detached houses had been built in Gidea Park, a short distance from the (then) small market town of Romford. There were fields opposite, and the house of their choice had a good-sized garden, surrounded by a thick privet hedge, with a stout childproof gate.

Poor Mother, who had longed to exchange neighbours for animals and country life, found she had jumped out of the frying pan into the fire. The new neighbours were mostly of her generation, but class distinction was still the order of the day – only this time *her* family was to be the one discriminated against.

The secluded garden was to become her refuge, and an endless source of play opportunities for my sister and me.

I was born fifteen months after the wedding, and the intervening time was devoted to curtain making, gardening and generally creating a home. For the next two and a half years the morning was devoted to 'jobs', and the afternoon to 'walking out'. Every afternoon Mother met another mother, who became her soul mate, and who also had a baby six months older than me, and they pushed their prams, and walked and talked until teatime. Two and half years later they both had second babies, so two mothers, two babies and two toddlers did the familiar round up and down and round the neighbourhood.

I loved every minute of it, and knew exactly when I wanted to be pushed to enjoy the view of the gardens from a height, and when I wanted to walk to view the scene from ground level. My favourite walking stretch was along the railings at the foot of the railway bank. A huge blackberry bush grew there, and the wind blew rubbish through the railing and into the bush where it was caught up in the thorny trails of the blackberry, and you never knew what you were going to see. Pink and blue bus tickets, some bright and new, some old and faded; cigarette packets, some of them with pictures of a bearded man looking through a white circle (a life belt, I learned later); pieces of paper, some speared by thorns and fluttering like butterflies trying to get free. But best of all were pieces of silver paper, some scrunched up into a ball, sometimes in a smooth piece straight from a chocolate bar or a cigarette packet, but they all caught the sun and shone magically.

Sometimes we went on a solo trip to Romford on Market Day, and that was best of all. The stalls were awash with colour: rolls of material, boxes of plants, rows of pinafores swinging from their hangers, piles of fruit and vegetables, china and fish. And each stall had a paraffin flare, which was lit on foggy days, or towards late afternoon. The stallholders were loud and jolly, telling us to "Walk up! Walk up!" and everything they offered was "Loverlee!"

One thing I remember very clearly: some stallholders were women and they shouted as loudly as the men, but there was a huge difference between men and women talking and men and women shouting their wares. Men and women talking indoors were not so very different, but the duets of shouting in the market were exciting in a particular sort of way.

Some of the shops were very small and crowded, and we had to be left in the pram outside, with the brakes clicked firmly on, while Mother went inside. We sat one each end, with our feet in the deep well between us, and as Mother emerged with the shopping she packed it under our seats. On one occasion she came out first with a bottle, which was stowed firmly at the back of the well, and then she went back for more. I was people-watching when suddenly I was aware of a trickle of wet running across the pavement; it wasn't raining, so where was it coming from? My eyes followed it back and I saw with horror that it started under the pram – I knew it had to be the bottle, but I was panic stricken that passers-by would think it was a huge, and ever growing, puddle of my making. I tried to scramble out, to dissociate myself from it, but people dashed to hold me safe, whereupon I thought they were going to grab me in anger. Truly awful!

Mother emerged at the crucial moment, calm and courteous as ever, thanking everyone, retrieving the bottle, and restoring smiles all round. The shopkeeper came out in his khaki overall, with an armful of newspapers and mopped up the pram and the pavement. The paraffin was replaced, and we departed, smelling horrendously.

I can still recapture the episode in vivid detail; if I could draw I could reproduce the exact setting. The smell of paraffin can still bring it all back sometimes: the background sound of the market in full swing, with buses trundling by, cows mooing at the far end of the market, and the close-up sound of people's anxious cries as they closed in on me – but above all my feelings as mild interest in the general scene turned to a sharp focus on the 'wet', the study of the trail, the momentary satisfaction as I discovered the place of origin, turning to panic as I realized my predicament, then anxiety as people converged upon me – and the relief of Mother coming to the rescue.

On looking back this is the memory above almost all others that makes me so certain now that early sensory development is of paramount importance in children's lives – it links things together, gives them meaning, and slowly leads towards an understanding that actions have consequences. Observation is the key, and when everything is so new, repetition is of the essence until the unfamiliar becomes familiar. Time spent watching is crucial so that every tiny detail registers.

I have no idea whether or not my very high sensory recall is associated with my dyslexia. It may be that given the opportunity all children could develop in this way, or it may be that it is some part of a compensatory development in my brain to offset whatever it was that made me dyslexic.

Be that as it may, I still believe that all children could benefit from a quiet, peaceful early start in life to give them unlimited time to watch, and touch, and listen, and hear the natural sounds of daily life, and smell the smells of daily life indoors and outside, and pit their strength against things to lift and pull and squeeze.

I doubt very much whether I would have been able to cope with later difficulties, which I didn't even understand, if it hadn't been for the slow pace, daily repetition (the same but always just that little bit different) and feeling of safety that these early years gave me.

Beginning to learn about people

I learned my own lessons through neighbours and their children. My best friend Norah lived two doors away, with her mother, father, older sister Cynthia and mother's sister Auntie Dee. We took turns to knock on each other's doors to ask, "Please can Norah/Brenda come and play?"

Different households – atmospheres and attitudes

I liked it best when Norah came to our house. Her own house was dark and unnaturally still, not a flutter of a curtain at tightly shut windows, not a displacement of a cushion, not a sound or smells from the kitchen. And yet the absence of smells had a smell of its own. It didn't smell of anything but neither did it smell fresh; the air just seemed dead and flat, and the first thing I did on my way home was to take deep breaths of fresh air.

We had to play in the same room as her mother and aunt, who were gentle, kind and benevolent, but nevertheless they watched us. And we had to play 'nicely'; it would have been unthinkable to move furniture around to make a home from which to play Mothers and Fathers. Also there was no colour anywhere. Walls, doors and even ceilings were vaguely brownish, and so were the rugs and curtains, and the layers of jumpers, skirts and woolly shawls that both these tiny women wore. Both had gold-rimmed spectacles, and grey hair in a small bun at the back, and fawnish skins, but both smiled a lot with genuine sweetness. I wasn't comfortable and neither, I think, was Norah. She was always nervous and anxious. When Norah came to our house she was still nervous at first, but gradually became more at home, and smiled and talked more.

What we both loved was for her to draw and me to watch. She was exceptionally gifted at drawing, especially horses of every kind: cart horses, hunters, sea-side donkeys, horse drawn carts and milk floats, horses jumping, racing, rolling on their backs. I would say, "Can you draw a horse that is....?" and whatever I suggested, she did, with the speed of lightning, and I never, ever grew tired of watching her. I remember saying, "Is she going to be an artist when she grows up?" and her mother laughing fondly as she said, "No, no, there isn't any money in that; she will have to have a proper job." Years later I met her in the street and recognised her at once. She hadn't changed a bit: still not able to stand tall and look up; still hesitant in her speech. I asked her what she did now and she said she was a nurse. I asked if she still drew wonderful horses, and she said she hadn't drawn anything for years. This grieves me to this day. I wonder why she was still so lacking in confidence, and why she hadn't chosen to exercise her remarkable talent just for her own pleasure.

Some people always build you up; others put you down

One day Norah and I were having a lovely morning making paper clothes for two cut-out cardboard dolls. We had decided on a new outfit for each doll, and mine was going to be a party frock. If ever there was wishful thinking, this was it! There were bows and puff sleeves, a sash with tassels, and frills from waist to the hem. I don't remember the colours of the bodice, but I do remember that I was revelling in colouring alternate frills of pink and blue. I was still working on them when Cynthia came to collect Norah. She looked over my shoulder briefly before saying, "You can't put pale blue and pink together. It's common." I had no idea what she meant, but I do know that something in her voice shattered all my joy and satisfaction.

Being different

As we had breakfast each morning there came a moment that Pauline and I looked forward to with unfailing interest. Suddenly the paths and the road would be awash with a tide of dark-suited men wearing bowler hats and carrying rolled umbrellas and leather briefcases. They strode purposefully by, starting with a trickle, becoming a great wave, and then tailing off until the last of all came Rosalie's daddy almost running and eating his breakfast toast. Upon enquiry we were told that they were all going to the station to catch a train to go to work in London. We asked where they worked and what they did, and it sounded truly dreadful: shut indoors all day, with the lights on if it was dark or foggy. And then, about six o'clock, they all trooped back again, more slowly now and no longer sprightly.

Father was home from the farm early in winter as soon as he had loaded the carts with produce, roped them securely, and sent them on their way to the Borough Market just over London's Tower Bridge, each in charge of their own horseman.

In summer it could be any time up to 10 o'clock if the harvest was in full swing, and he came home terribly tired and dusty, but elated if all was going well.

But there were quite a lot of days when he parked the car in the lock-up garage near the station, and joined the homeward trek. He stood out so clearly. On cold days he wore his heavy farm boots, old army puttees wound round his legs below the knee to keep his trousers from flapping in the mud, his great big all-enveloping greenish coat, a tweed cap pulled well down over his ears and eyebrows, and gauntlet gloves. Under one arm was a homemade crate holding bottles of milk, and in the other hand a small sack, emblazoned in scarlet, 'S. Gunary & Sons', holding perhaps a couple of cabbages, some carrots and turnips, and possibly some oranges from the Borough Market.

In the summer he wore stout shoes, flannel trousers, a sweat stained shirt with rolled-up sleeves, and an ancient panama hat. This time the sack contained lettuces, radishes, tomatoes, new potatoes and perhaps a basket of soft fruit. All the year round his face, hands, and arms were sun and wind burned, and whatever he wore he looked wonderfully cuddly.

He was, we told each other, easily the best of the bunch. How could you cuddle up to someone pale and dark-suited? (Easily, of course, if he was your father!) But I can see so clearly now why we thought he was so special, and why others thought he simply didn't belong.

One day I thought I would go round to the big block of flats where I knew Petronella lived, and ask her to play with me, something I had never done before. Her father was very grand indeed, the Mace Bearer for the Lord Mayor of London, no less. After the Lord Mayor's Show there would be pictures in the paper of the Procession. We loved the ceremony − the carriages and horses, the velvet robes, frilly lace cuffs over hands, three-cornered hats adorned with feathers, massive gold chains round necks, and gleaming swords. We played Lord Mayor's Shows for weeks afterwards − and were greatly in awe of the fact that Petronella went to the fancy dress party the Lord Mayor gave for the children of his staff. At least, at one level we were aware of all this, but on this occasion I just wanted someone to play with and I made no connection between the little girl I saw in the road from time to time and this exalted background.

I climbed the outside iron staircase to the top floor where I knew she lived, and rang the bell. Petronella opened the door and said, "Yes?" and I asked if she would like to come and play. She said, "No, I am not allowed to." I asked why not and she said, "Because Daddy says I mustn't play with you because you are common. Your father is only a farmer," and the door was shut. She had been perfectly nice and friendly, and I didn't feel in the least hurt or upset, just completely baffled.

Gradually friends fell away, often much to the children's regret but the parents were adamant. As so few of them understood and entered into our kind of play, it didn't really matter. Mother, Pauline and I were left to our own very happy devices. Occasionally we visited, and were visited by, Mother and Father's oldest friends and their children, and they were always lovely people who got on splendidly together. We knew nothing about 'class' but most certainly we knew about people who felt 'right' for us and those who didn't.

On looking back, this was one of greatest bonuses of our young lives. Far from withdrawing from the world, or being shunned by it, we had withdrawn into the world of nature, play, and the jobs that had to be done on a daily, weekly or seasonal basis, but above all the endless play of real childhood.

Self-protection

Mother never judged anybody; she just explained them. And as her own instincts were so good, she allowed us to develop our own and to trust them. This has been of inestimable value all of my life.

When I consider the later problems of dyslexia, about which I knew nothing at the time, it seems to me that quite often I used instinct to guide me. One of the things I needed to guard against was exposure to ridicule, accusations and failure, for it is difficult to function if you are burdened by guilt and low self-esteem. I may be quite wrong about this but I can forgive myself for lying and cheating, for I always knew so clearly why I was doing it, and back-checked with Mother, who helped me to see that it was usually fear of the person concerned that gave rise to this subterfuge. If people were kind and patient I didn't need to protect myself, as I could just listen and take on board what was said. She didn't condone lying; she just took some of the burden and guilt away.

A usual 'cheat' was to write very small or very badly if I didn't know how to spell something. If the teacher said with exasperation, "I've told you time and time again that it is 'e' not 'a'," I would intervene and say, "I'm sorry, my writing is very bad, but that was *meant* to be an 'e'." Sometimes I got away with it, sometimes not – but in any event I continued not to remember the right spelling.

Another 'cheat' was to copy someone's work if I knew that I hadn't a hope of understanding, or to say that I had hurt my wrist and hadn't been able to do whatever it was, or to say that I felt sick and ask to go home. Sometimes I would brazen it out. In General Knowledge one day the question was, "What does 'quarantine' mean?" I said it was the name of an early apple, but as soon as I heard the proper answer I knew that the apple in Grandma's orchard was a 'quaranden', but I stuck to my guns, and had to be given a tick because the teacher couldn't disprove what I said.

Dyslexia is quite enough to battle against without the battle for morality, too – there were times when I felt as though I was battling simultaneously on so many fronts that I just might burst or sink without trace.

But all these difficulties were to come later, once I was at school. Before school there were no problems at all, except that sometimes I longed to break the barriers of Mother's gentleness, patience and restraint. When we reached the park and were let off our reins, I remember running and running until I fell panting to the ground – just like the carthorses let out into the field after work. They too galloped, and rolled, and shook their bridle-free heads before settling down peacefully. Being able to talk about my feelings from a very early age was tremendously helpful.

I tried to pass all this on to our children, and am glad to remember our three-year-old son saying, after a particular caller had left, "I don't like her – she talks with her mouff." I knew exactly what he meant: there was no personal connection. There were just words that conformed to social rules about not ignoring the children, but nothing was said that Simon could recognise as being for him personally.

I dread to think what a muddle I would have been in if Mother had tried to 'help' by indulging in teaching-talk during the pre-school years: talk about numbers, and colours, and words denoting space, size and weight. All this can wait. But simple honesty, understanding, example and explanation about our growing relationships with other people, and with ourselves, can't wait – it is part of the bedrock of our lives.

One day as I was watching Mother gardening, a long worm suddenly appeared in the newly dug earth. I don't remember feeling anything other than surprise, and when I asked what it was the answer was 'a worm', and she picked it up and put it in the palm of her hand.

It was astonishing. This strange object drew both ends in until it became short and fat and then, as the supporting hand stayed still, it stretched itself out until it became long and thin. When the moving end reached the edge of the hand it waved about a bit as if looking to see where to go, but it hadn't got any eyes as far as I could see, so it drew back to safety and became short and fat again. Mother held it up carefully by its middle, and it was even more amazing: it wriggled, and as it twisted and turned I could see more colours than I had thought at first. The colours shaded from dark brown to lightish pinky-brown, and there were purple streaks as well.

I said, "Are you going to keep it, or throw it away?" and the answer was, "Neither. We are going to put it back in the ground because worms are *very* valuable. They tunnel through the earth and let the air in, and they break up the lumps and hard bits of earth so that it is loose enough for the roots of the plants to push through." I got the picture exactly, and it was enough for the time being. I asked if it was going back where it had come from, and was told, "No, because I don't want to damage it with my spade, so would you like to put it back on a patch of earth that has already been dug?" I said I would and reached out quite naturally to pick it up and carry it off, having watched it long enough for surprise to turn to interest, and then to concern for the worm. On being put down, the worm began to wriggle over the surface of the soft earth, and then to burrow down out of sight, presumably to start making more tunnels. All *most* satisfactory.

Years later at school we were helped to make a wormery in a large glass tank. We put in layers of earth and sand, and then the teacher put the worms on top (because of the 'ugh!' factor among the on-lookers). We watched them tunnel their way out of sight, and then went and sat down at our desks. Over the following days and weeks the clear-cut light and dark layers in the tank began to become blurred as the worms tunnelled through, eating earth and sand at one end and excreting it at the other. Sometimes we could see them as they pressed against the glass, and we could watch them wriggling along. I found it quite interesting because it illustrated what I already knew, but it was only a mild interest.

Even now if I hear the word 'wormery', I have a flash-back to a classroom: wood floors, wooden desks and chairs, windows shut, air smelling of the class-room smell that stays with us forever. And there is the glass tank, sitting on a table by the window — not as good as a garden, but much better than books alone.

But if I hear the word 'worms' it is all so different. I am there in fresh air, my hands in the soil that has a feel and smell that also stays with us forever. There is space, and freedom, and freshness, and silence and joy, and the worms are my gardening friends.

My heart still goes out to the mother I encountered on a playgroup course. She was a country girl who had married and gone to live in a flat in a tower block, and she was absolutely determined that her children would not miss out on her own most treasured memories. She had window boxes that she planted up and watered with the children's help. She put strips of trellis up the side walls of the balcony and the children planted nasturtiums to climb up, and she had a washing-up bowl of earth from her mum's garden. At each visit she carried a large biscuit tin of fresh earth back to the flat, and the children transferred it to an emptied washing-up bowl. Sometimes the earth was dry, sometimes wet and heavy after rain, and the children searched for worms, or small beetles, or ants, or wood lice that would curl up into a ball if touched. Worms were transferred to the window boxes; any other small creatures were put in a jar and carried downstairs to be tipped out on the grass. At her next visit home the old earth was taken back to the garden, and a new tin-full replaced it. And then the children made mud-pies in the remaining earth. What more could anyone do to put children in touch with nature?

Other vivid memories centre around ants. You never knew where you were going to find them, and often it was they who found you first. You would be lying on the grass, and suddenly become aware of the lightest of ticklings, running hap-hazard along your legs. You sat up to inspect, and there was an ant, or several of them, scuttling like mad with

34

no apparent purpose – up to your knee, down into your white canvas shoes or darting from nowhere to disappear under your dress or shorts and upwards where you absolutely knew you didn't want them. You jumped up and tried to brush them all off with your hands, and they transferred themselves to your hand and began to run dementedly up and down your arm. They tickled mostly, but occasionally one would bite or sting, or did whatever it was that made a small but definite pricking sensation.

Sometimes the ants were minute and pale amber in colour, or they could be slightly longer and darker, or larger still with a much fiercer capacity to bite or sting. And rarest of all, but definitely to be avoided, were the even bigger flying ants. Sometimes a line of ants appeared crossing a path like soldiers on parade, and then we tried to trace where they came from, and where they were going to – if it was into the house then we told whichever parent we found first, and action was taken. There was a clear liquid that was smeared on a piece of flat glass and put in the pathway of the brigade of ants. The theory was that they would pick up the poison on their feet and carry it back into the anthill that was their home, where it would kill all the other ants. How many were killed we had no way of knowing, but we were always deeply impressed to see an immediate exodus from the ant hill in a new direction, almost every ant carrying a huge egg seemingly as big as itself. We understood why they had to be killed, or forced to move, for if they got into the house they made their way straight to the pantry, and sugar bowls, treacle tins, opened jam jars and cake tins would be swarming with them. And in the garden they burrowed away in the soil, pushing fine earth up, which formed a mound so big that it sometimes smothered small rock plants. They created such a network of passages underground that the root hairs of plants were left dangling in space, until they dried out and could no longer send water and plant food up to the plant above.

I realise that I am still hazy about whether ants bite or sting (bite would be my guess), and I couldn't draw a large ant with the right number of legs, or be accurate about the head in relation to the segments of its anatomy – they always moved too quickly for observation to be accurate. But what I know very well indeed is the 'antfulness' of ants, and I would feel I had been cheated if I only knew about ants from books and diagrams.

Bees and wasps were familiar, and I absolutely knew that both sting because I had been stung several times. Grandma taught us to look carefully to see which it was that had delivered the sting, because the stings needed different treatment – a wasp sting needed vinegar (I remembered this by connecting mental pictures to the waspish, or vinegary, old busy-bodies of books), and bee stings needed a rub with a lump of washing soda. These days, antihistamines are the order of the day for either, but I am oddly glad that I knew originally about the acidity or alkalinity of the stings. I knew, too, that the wasp jabbed its sting in, injected its poison, then withdrew its sting and flew away – because I had watched it happen on the back of my hand once. I also knew, and felt it was a kind of poetic justice, that the bee couldn't remove its sting so it remained sticking in me and the bee went away to die. I had seen the sting left in me, and remember the injunction, "Don't pull it out, just brush it off sideways. If you pull it out you will squeeze the tiny bulb that contains the poison, and pump a bit more into you."

I am glad I learned all this at first hand and was clear about many differences between bees and wasps. I am glad, too, that I learned from observation that bees buzzed about all summer long, burrowing into the centre of the flowers, coating their legs with golden pollen, and then transferring it to their backs so that they could carry it off to the beehive, where it was converted into honey. Sometimes we had jars of clear runny honey from the shop, and sometimes it was thick and more difficult to spread and sometimes we had a honeycomb from Grandad's beehive, and then we could see how the bees stored the honey they made − in the thinnest of wax compartments, attached to the light wooden frames provided for them by all beekeepers.

Wasps, on the other hand, didn't make much of an appearance until the late summer and autumn − and woe betide anyone who picked up windfall apples or plums, and conveyed them straight to their mouths without turning them over gingerly to see if there were any wasps half-hidden in the holes they had eaten away. This was one of the lessons that we learned through fear. We knew that stings on our hands, or arms, or bare feet or almost anywhere else were unpleasant, but nothing to worry about usually − but if a wasp got into our mouths then the swelling from the sting on the tongue, or the roof of the mouth, would swell up so much that it would block our throats until we couldn't breathe. And we would die.

Two things followed from this; one, it made us extremely careful in picking up fruit from the ground or off the trees or bushes; two, it made us panicky if wasps were in the vicinity while we ate picnics or had meals in the garden. Fear leading to caution is good; fear leading to panic can be counter-productive.

Parents and grandparents taught us how to proceed with caution. No, we didn't have to eat inside with doors and windows shut, but neither did we have to jump up and down waving our arms and shouting, "A wasp! A wasp!" as we ate outside. Grandma used to put a spoonful of jam, and some vinegar to ferment it, in a jam jar that had its lid pierced with a hole big enough for a wasp to find its way in, but too small for it to fly out again. As we carried food outside to put on the old garden table Grandma would hold up the jam jar saying, "This one is for the wasps. Who is going to carry it out?" We clamoured for the honour, and spent the meal not in a state of panic, but in a gleeful watchfulness to see what the wasps did. Those that found their way in got drunk on the fermented mixture and drowned, and when two inches or so of liquid in the jar was full of wasps it had to be dealt with. I was glad when the wasps went in, but then remember not wanting to watch them drown – should we let them go again at the end of the meal? Grandma had the solution. There was no triumph or rejoicing, just, "Now we'll dig a little hole and tip them in," and as the hole was filled it was, "There, they can't sting anybody now."

Consider the word 'play' in relation to all that we learned about, and from, wasps. Yes, we loved to pick up windfalls; yes, we loved to have throwing competitions with the rotten ones; yes, we loved to eat the good bits of the apples; yes, we enjoyed carting windfalls to the compost heap; yes, we enjoyed pretending we were farmers, or park keepers, or gardeners who had been given the job of clearing the lawn before the Queen came to tea. The play was endless, and constantly changing direction as ideas flooded in. But then came a wasp sting, and off we went for comfort. Play was forgotten as we tuned in to the explanation of what had happened, and what we could do about it – think of this as the discipline of consequence. *If* I pick up windfalls or eat an ice cream carelessly, *then* I may be stung; *therefore* I need to know what to do about it if I am stung, and also how to prevent it happening again if possible. This is not only training in First Aid; it is also an early lesson in understanding that if we can do something to deal with a mishap and prevent a similar one, we begin to feel that we have some decree of control over our fear. We all need this, all through our lives.

Then there is the question of morality, which is essential to us all at any age. Can I kill *indiscriminately* to safeguard myself? No. My conscience (developed from parents and grandparents) enables me, under some circumstances, to kill anything that threatens me, or those who are my responsibility – but I won't go round the house or garden killing wantonly. If I kill, will it be with exaltation, giving me an inflated sense of being in control? No, but neither will it be with guilt or remorse, though it may sometimes be with regret; it is a balanced judgement, and learning starts with early childhood experiences – it can't be left to the lessons in Nature Study, First Aid, Sex, Citizenship or Ethics at school, important though those are.

Learning about plants

Nature study at school was where I came into my own, as I found I knew it already. Sitting there in my desk, with my hand shooting up at every question, was balm to the soul after all the struggles and failures. Inability to spell all the words that poured out didn't trouble me, and quite possibly the spelling wasn't as bad as it might have been if I had stopped constantly to debate with myself which letters I wanted, in which order. Another bonus was that I was quite good at drawing, and often all I had to do was put my knowledge on paper in that form, and then add arrows and labels.

I didn't know how I knew, and certainly I had never been taught at home as teachers teach in schools. But on looking back I see quite clearly that my knowledge of plants came about as I watched Mother gardening. Like most children I had a naturally good eye for colour, beauty and texture, a good nose for smell (be it the scent of flowers or horse manure), and a good ear for sound, from thunder to dry leaves underfoot or the popping of gorse pods on a hot summer day. This is an excellent start in life, and I truly grieve that today's constant background music and manufactured toys blunt the sensory development that every child needs.

However, back to 'nature study'. Apart from looking at and smelling flowers with delight, I experimented. Fat peony buds reached the point of beginning to reveal the colour hidden by their green sepals and it seemed only kind to help them on their way by peeling back the sepals to reveal the tight red bud underneath. But, disappointingly, my kindness killed them. The crumpled balls of red petals stayed exactly as they were, and finally turned black and crumbled to the touch; the buds that had escaped my attention grew fatter and fatter, and slowly unfurled of their own accord into glorious full-blown flowers. As far as I can remember I never did it again, but neither have I ever stopped a child making the same mistake, for the "I wonder what would happen if……?" stage of learning is valuable. If children don't ask themselves questions they can't find out the answers; if we tell them not to, even if we explain why, there is never quite the same certainty as arises from doing it.

I learned about roots by watching Mother tip market plants out of their pots with such care, and transfer them to their prepared holes, then she poured a little rainwater into the hole, and waited for it to drain away before carefully filling up the remaining space with the surrounding loose soil, giving it a gentle press all round, and finally a last drink. I must have watched this process dozens of times, standing or kneeling beside her in companionable silence. I didn't ask questions, and she didn't volunteer any information. She enjoyed having her hands in the earth and planting everything with meticulous care, and I enjoyed watching and taking in every deft movement of her tools and hands.

She was playing. I knew this was so because after she had done all that needed to be done in the house she would say, "If anyone wants me I'm playing in the garden." I understand this exactly. It meant she was doing exactly what she wanted to do, and was loving every minute of it. And I watched, sharing the peace and the purpose.

Eventually when we were in the market one day I asked if I could have a plant, and in response to being asked, "What would you like?" I said, "A pansy" and was told to choose one. It took forever! Once you start to look at their faces you see how different they all are – in the box they are just 'pansies', but being asked to pick one was entirely different.

I don't remember what colour I chose, but I do remember planting it. After all those hours of watching it should surely only have taken a couple of minutes, but doing for yourself what you have seen someone else doing so often is altogether different.

I dug the hole, but when I put the potted plant beside it I could see that it wasn't big enough, so more trowel work was called for. Then I tried to tip the pansy out of its pot, but my hand wasn't big enough to hold it, and it fell into the hole in a heap. I picked it up with two hands and squeezed it to stop the crumbling – and Mother said, "Be careful of the roots." Roots? What roots? That was the first time I had thought of a flower having something important underneath the ground. I was shown the little white threads looking like cotton, and learned that at the end of each little thread there were root-hairs so fine that they couldn't even be seen – but these were the little hairs that picked up the water and the plant food that had to be sent up to the leaves and stem to feed them, and to make the buds and the flowers. If the hairs were damaged they couldn't do their work, and they wouldn't grow again, so we needed to damage them as little as possible.

This knowledge and understanding stayed with me, and when formal lessons began and I learned the words *osmotic pressure* and *capillary attraction*, it all fell into place and enriched what I had already learned during those years of watching an activity in the garden.

I remember another experiment with planting. Outside the back door was the dustbin, and beside it the pile of ash that came from the coal fire and boiler each day and was used on paths to fill in holes that collected puddles. One day I looked at the dustbin and the pile of ash, and thought how ugly it was, so I set about improving things. I spread the ash over a wide patch beside and round the dustbin and it looked like a grey flowerbed, except that there were no flowers. I took a trowel and pail over the road and went into the field that had a broad band of weeds between the paths and the crop. Big plants like thistles and nettles pricked and stung and were left alone, and tufts of grass were not what I wanted, but the pretty little white flowers with feathery leaves were perfect – I knew they were called 'poisonous daises', but I just thought that was their name and made no connections at all. I dug up half a bucketful, took it home, and set about planting my new patch. I remember thinking how pretty it looked, and how pleased my parents would be, but it didn't work out like that at all.

It just so happened that Father saw it first, and he was angry because I should have known better than to handle poisonous plants – had I eaten any part of any plant? Had I eaten anything else before washing my hands? He was filled with fears for my sister and me, and had a particular concern for poisonous plants (deadly nightshade, hemlock, foxgloves, yew, laburnums and laurel berries), dangerous substances (quick lime, red lead, dressings for seeds and pesticides), and 'germs' (lock jaw being the prime suspect, not without reason since a horseman and a great Shire horse had died in two separate incidents). Mother had all the same concerns but approached them in a different way – we were never to eat any berries, or parts of any plants, without checking with her first that they were safe; we were never to go near any of the tins or jars in the veterinary cupboard or the shed where farm poisons were locked; and we were never to go near any of the men who were using sprays or dusts on any of the crops. I don't remember having any problem with these rules; we had so few that when a dire warning was given in all seriousness about anything, we accepted and obeyed.

However, on the occasion of my lovely surprise-garden, things went from bad to worse. Surely I knew that nothing would grow in dead ash? I simply hadn't thought in terms of 'soil' being dead or alive, and when I began to cry he called me "a watery headed little cabbage!" This makes him sound an ogre, but he wasn't. He loved all little things – calves, kittens, puppies, babies and young children – and he couldn't bear them to be hurt, let alone killed. Allied to this was his habitual silence, and a complete inability to handle emotion. It was a combination Mother handled beautifully, and it didn't affect my sister, who had a heart murmur and called forth his gentleness at all times, but he and I were a recipe for upsets, shouting and tears. He was the world's worst teacher, but I always knew he loved me, and that we were all absolutely safe in his overall care, so somehow everything was all right.

The plants died, of course, but the learning stayed with me.

In complete contrast, my earliest memories of strawberries are of watching Grandma in the big farmhouse kitchen preparing for her annual haymaking strawberry teas. The strawberries were rinsed under running water in the big kitchen colander and tipped on to a cloth to dry before being put into a basket lined with strawberry leaves. Castor sugar was put into a pudding basin, with a white crochet cover weighted by a border of china beads to keep the flies off. Stacks of bread and butter sandwiches were cut (slices of bread and butter were bound to fall face-down in the dust of the hay field, but dropped sandwiches could be dusted off and eaten). Another covered pudding basin held cream, skimmed off last night's wide pan of milk and cooled on the slate slabs of the north-facing pantry. Tea was made in the largest teapot, and milk and homemade lemonade were put into any empty stoppered bottles that came to hand.

Two large rugs were gathered up, and Grandma's sunshade, then off we all traipsed to the hay field, where the last of the hay had been cut, and the men were tossing the drying hay into small haycocks. Grandma's sons continued working, but their wives and children, Grandma's staunch kitchen helper and anyone else who happened to be there all set about making a couch for Grandma, with her sunshade in position, and the aunties. One rug was spread out for us assorted children.

Sandwiches were passed round, and the bowls of strawberries, sugar and cream. We picked up a strawberry by its green hull, dipped it in the cream, then the sugar, and stuffed it in our mouths, before the best bits had dribbled away. Bliss! Long before everything had been eaten, the cream had made the sugar wet and lumpy, and whiskers of hay had got into both. The midges had bitten us to pieces, and the dried grass stalks had tickled and pricked our legs and thighs. Milk, tea and lemonade had been spilled – and none of it mattered. If one of us had a particularly messy accident, Grandma would clap her hands on her knees in delight and say, "Bless the child!" No one was cross, no one cried, no one complained – it was Grandma's Hay Field Strawberry Tea, to be savoured and remembered forever.

Fortunately, the experience of strawberry picnics continues for some in fields where people can Pick Your Own, and these picnics too I remember with pleasure. Sun beating down on my back, glistening red berries on clear golden straw, skylarks singing their hearts out so far above us that they are out of sight, and fingers red-stained with strawberry juice. On one of our last such days together, my husband and I were in a field where there was no sight or sound of anything other than the field and its surrounding trees and the skylarks. Suddenly a mother, father and child of about five appeared, and the child was beside herself with wonder and joy. She darted from row to row as extra large strawberries caught her eye, and she was calling out, "Daddy, look at this one! And this one... and *this* one!" Daddy replied with an appreciative, "Yes!" and "That's a beauty!" while her mother kept saying, "Ssh! Be quiet. Don't shout," in increasingly loud commands. I called out to her, "Please don't worry about us. It's lovely to hear her excitement. Is it the first time she has seen a whole field of strawberries, with permission to pick as many as she likes?" Mother said it was, and I said no wonder she was so happy and excited. I hoped it would release her from wanting her child to behave thoughtfully, but sadly it didn't. The background nag of, "Ssh! Be quiet! Stop shouting...." continued. No wonder it was to Daddy she turned to share her joy. If only that mother had suddenly stood still, head tilted upwards, and said, "Listen!" that child might have heard the skylarks. If only .....

Children's personal experience, with *time* to savour it, is invaluable, but it is heightened or lessened by the messages they receive from the adults who may also be involved. Am I being good, or naughty? Does this give them as much pleasure as it is giving me? Am I going to be given all the time I want and need, or is it going to be cut short with the usual, "Hurry up! Here, let me help you...."? Am I going to be given as much silence as I need, or are there going to be endless questions and directions? Do they realise that every single day I am seeing, and trying to do, things that I have never, ever seen or done in my life before?

All this vital learning starts long before school, and the sum total of all these experiences and values is the foundation for 'The Family' that is talked about so glibly.

Action for its own sake

When I was about eight, my friend Norah used to call for me on a Sunday afternoon, and together we went to Sunday school. I liked the responsibility of us being allowed to go on our own; I liked the order and formality of the service; I liked trying to find hymns from the board high on the wall in front of us (I never could bridge that gap, but I still liked to try before looking to see which page Norah had found); I loved the singing; I loved the lilt and simplicity of the beautiful Biblical language. All these things went together most pleasingly – but then came the sermon. I simply couldn't relate to this, even when it was in story form, because it was delivered in a strange voice that bore no relation to ordinary people speaking to each other. So I counted windowpanes, and the people in front of me (I knew it would be rude to turn round) and the number of rows of pews they sat in; and I looked at the hats, and the altar cloths, and the vicar's clothes. But above all, if it was sunny, I followed the glorious colours flooding through the stained glass, and watched to see where they alighted, and what they did to the space in between: then, as now, I could feel my whole inner self lift up with joy at beholding colour.

And then, one unexceptional day, something happened that I have never forgotten. The Vicar slowly mounted the stairs to the pulpit, looked down quietly as we settled, then gave us the reference to the book and chapter from which he was going to preach – nothing unusual so far. But then came the 'happening'. He said, "The text for today is, 'I am come that ye might have life, and have it more abundantly'." I can't begin to describe the impact of those few words – they summed up everything I wanted and needed, had always wanted and needed, and still do. I had always consciously *loved* the feeling of being alive, in every possible way, and finding a use for all that energy that flowed through my arms, hands and legs – and the bit inside my head that seemed to draw the outside and inside together, and to direct it.

Abundant. Abundantly. What wonderful words! I had never heard them before, and I didn't have to ask what they meant (still less have someone simplify them for me); they said it all in one glorious rounded burst of sound. *That's* what I wanted, and that is what I have had, and so enjoyed, all my life – even when there have been times when it was distress and suffering that were abundant.

Pendulums always swing equally, to and fro, between the extremes – we can't have one without the other.

I remember with clarity and satisfaction inventing a kind of mini training circuit, just for the sheer joy of doing it.

My sister and I shared a double bed in a small back bedroom; there was a window running along one wall, with a window sill and a window at either end that opened – and stayed open as far or as little as you liked, according to where you fixed the hinged arm of the window on to a small metal stump in the middle of the window frame. The window at one end looked straight down onto the dustbin outside the back door, but the window at the other end looked down on to a corrugated tin roof over the coal, and the chopping block for splitting fire wood. Both were hidden from the garden beyond by a creeper-covered trellis.

One day, as I looked out at the garden, and the neighbouring gardens on three sides of ours, I suddenly had an idea. (My ideas were always sudden, and no sooner registered than acted upon!) I felt sure I could get out of the window, drop onto the tin roof, slither down the roof to the gutter, and drop down onto the lawn. At once, I put the plan into action. First step, put the bedroom chair under the window so that I could climb onto the window sill; second step, open the window as far as possible – in fact, don't latch it at all, just fold it right back flat onto the wall; third step, get out of the window and drop onto the roof – ah! well now, just how?

Funnily enough, although I couldn't 'do' maths, I always loved problem solving – as long as I could do it by trial and error.

Every time I see children on climbing apparatus, I empathise with their struggles and dilemmas. Head through first? No, not safe. One leg through first? Could be, but what happens next? No good sitting astride the windowsill if I can't get the other leg through – and there doesn't seem to be much room to manoeuvre. One knee on the windowsill, and pull the other one through somehow? Not enough room without risking the glass of the fixed middle windows.

What was I actually aiming to do? Sit on the windowsill, with my back to the bedroom, and push off so that I jumped down facing the garden? No, the drop was too high for comfort. What then? I needed to be face down on the windowsill, with my head in the bedroom, and my legs dangling down outside. Then I could lower myself to the full extent of my arms, and drop down onto the roof, which wouldn't be too far. I tried that, but ouch! The metal window-fixer spike stuck into my tummy – turn on your side, quick! I don't remember how I solved it, but I do remember very well indeed the confusion of hands, knees, feet, shoulders, neck and head as I tried. I have a vague memory of opening the wardrobe door and bringing it back until I could hold onto it, a vague feeling of standing on the windowsill, while I steadied myself as I tried to kneel with both knees on the window frame itself – one knee each side of the wretched stubby catch.

I have never been able to recall the eventual drill I organised for myself – but I do know I worked out exactly how I had to do it, and repeated it ever after.

Once the really tricky bit had been mastered, then it was plain sailing all the way. Native caution indicated that this was something Mother wouldn't allow. I understood how dangerous this would seem to her, but I 'knew' I could do it perfectly safely, if I followed my carefully-worked-out system. So I compromised – I would do it (safely), while she was having her after-lunch nap on the couch: then we would both be happy. What could be fairer or more sensible than that?

So every afternoon, as soon as she was asleep, I ran upstairs, got up on the window sill, accomplished the tricky bit, dropped down onto the tin roof, scrambled and slithered down to the edge, turned face down, eased myself over the gutter and dropped down to the lawn. What next? I turned left, dashed round the house to the front door, dashed (quietly) upstairs again, and repeated the process – only this time I turned right, and dashed round the house the other way. I repeated it, again and again, until my energy and excitement had worked themselves out – whereupon I lay panting on the bed. Did I fall asleep? I don't remember, but it would have been the natural thing to do, so I may have done.

Eventually, this entire exercise lost some of its thrill, so I thought on to the next stage. One of these days I might find myself escaping from enemy hordes, so it would be prudent to have another escape route, preferably from a ground floor window on the front of the house. The only option was the dining room, especially as there were good stout chairs to climb on. This time, with far less height to the ground, it seemed possible to do something else altogether – what if I sat on the window sill, and propelled myself forward in a clear jump? All went according to plan, except for one thing I really don't think I could have foreseen. I must have been under five, because when I went to school I had proper knickers bought from a shop. Before that, Mother made them, from Grandma's paper pattern, and they didn't have elastic (not good for children!). Instead they had a placket each side, and did up with two good strong linen-covered buttons, well sewn on.

Alas, the metal stump in the middle of the windowsill pierced the material, and as I pushed off there was a tearing sound, and I found myself suspended from the windowsill by the aforesaid band, strong buttons and buttonholes. I was well and truly stuck: I couldn't get back, and I couldn't get down to the ground. I just hung there. Nobody walked by, and I didn't know whether to be glad or not.

The next thing I remember is my sister Pauline being there – had she been watching throughout? Had she been having her afternoon nap, and woken up of her own accord? Had I called? It is all a blank, but I do remember saying, "Fetch Mummy!" and knowing that all would be well as soon as she arrived. I also remember her standing in the flower bed trying to lift me up off the catch, but I was too heavy; and the only alternative was to lift me up high enough to take the strain off the waist band, and to tell me to undo the buttons – then she could release the band from the stump, and complete the rescue. But as soon as she put me on the ground and took her arms away, the remnants of my knickers fell to the ground, and I was mortified!

I also remember she was very quiet throughout, and it wasn't her usual peaceful quietness. She didn't say a word, or ask a single question; she was just quiet in a very particular way – and I knew without question that my assumption that the secret climbing episodes were 'fair and sensible' had been wrong.

Something has just occurred to me, even as I write. If, instead of being born in 1920, to my particular parents, in our particular home with a garden, I had been born in the '90s, to stressed parents (or a single parent) living in a flat, or a smaller house with a tiny garden or back yard, and in a climate where young children can't go out to play in the park or streets alone – what then? I rather think I might have been diagnosed as being hyperactive, or having attention deficit disorder, and medically prescribed drugs to quieten me down. The thought frightens me very much.

I can see that for my poor parents and eventual teachers it would have been a blessed relief if I had been rendered easier to manage – but what about me? What of all my wonderful 'ideas'; my working out of problems, my mental and physical energy, and the ability to channel them through endless forms of creative play? What about all that glorious *abundance* artificially damped down?

I don't doubt for a moment that some children do indeed suffer from a genuine disorder, and need drugs, but not *all* of them, surely? How many are like me? Happy, eager, enthusiastic, with this strong urge to do things, make things, invent things – not 'naughty', but denied the opportunity to channel it all positively through the *real* play and work of childhood? What would have happened to me? I dread to think.

I suppose, eventually, I would have just given up in despair, and settled for watching television – at least my eyes would be occupied, and my ears, and my taste buds if I had enough to munch. But I think the time would have come when all that vitality would have burst through, and I could easily have run amuck, shouting, throwing things, breaking things – even my own most cherished possession, as a way of saying, "See if I care! What's the point of anything?"

Do I feel so strongly because I am dyslexic? Because I have always been so dependant on action and creativity, and living through my senses? Also, possibly, because so much of my childhood was spent on a farm? There, it becomes obvious that if too many animals are in a field or barn that is too small to give them each the space they need, then they attack each other, or bully and trample the weakest underfoot, or pluck each other's feathers out, or abort their babies, or simply fail to thrive.

I have had another uncomfortable thought. If my caged energy had managed to break through into positive action, eventually – then I think it might have been anti-authority in a big way.

When the Great Train Robbery hit the headlines, I remember being shocked to realise that I could have relished being one of the gang – the initial idea, the meticulous planning, the building of a hand-selected team with complementary skills and absolute discretion and trustworthiness. No, I could never have condoned, or taken part in, violence; neither could I have appropriated other people's property – yet even here, given a different parental up-bringing, I can understand how used bank notes might not seem to be in the same category as your household possessions, or my pension money being carried home from the Post Office. But violence and morality apart, the actual planning, the route-finding, the meticulous timing, the establishment of a safe house, the dove-tailing of it all – *that* I would have entered into wholeheartedly.

Anything, for me, would be preferable to feeling that I had been robbed of my energy, and of my chance to do something worthwhile every day of my life. How can you feel confident in your ability, your very *self*, if you feel judged and found wanting by the educational system, and sometimes even by your parents?

Whether or not children are dyslexic, whether or not they are academically intelligent, whether or not they are gifted in non-academic ways, we are all responsible for trying to give young children what *they* need in order to unfold, and to develop their own awareness and abilities, in loving security and personal space, during the precious early years.

And we must try to give parents the understanding help *they* need in trying to do this, when the odds are so stacked against them.

Drugs (with certain exceptions), and constant monitoring, testing and examination are not the answer – especially when we are tested on those things we can't do, without anybody discovering what we *can* do.

I like the saying, now prevalent, that the present educational system, with its emphasis on teaching things that can be measured by tests, is the equivalent of constantly weighing the pig without fattening it!

Dancing, music and mime

When I was three, something wonderful happened that enriched the rest of my life.

Our neighbour asked one day if we could take her daughter to her dancing class – so we did, pram pushing our way to The Hut (where everything happened) and making ourselves known.

The teacher explained that parents were not allowed to watch the dancing. (She wanted the children to be free from watchfulness, comparison, criticism or even praise, in order that they could discover for themselves the joy of moving to music.) However, as this was our first visit, we could stay if we didn't make a sound. So Mother sat quietly on the sidelines with the pram and me beside her.

It was magic from then on.

The children had bare feet and skimpy little tunics in all the colours of the rainbow, and they made no sound at all as they flowed round the room. A comfortable lady sat at the piano watching the dancers all the time, but her hands moved up and down the piano and the most wonderful music rippled out – it skipped and galloped, soothed and excited, sometimes soft and sometimes loud, but it changed what the children did!

The combination of music and movement was irresistible, and I slipped off the chair and joined in. I was aware of Mother reaching out to retrieve me, but I was off and away. The first time I passed the teacher, she caught me and removed my shoes; the second time she caught me and removed my socks – and that was when I discovered dancing, and I wanted it to go on forever.

At the end of the lesson I watched the rainbow fade to navy and brown as parents collected and dressed their children, but I also heard snippets of conversation above my head – something about "too young", and "if she wants to come back….." and, "Let's just see what happens – but don't make her a tunic yet; let her dance in her petticoat." (We all wore petticoats in those days, but without that clear directive I might well have been cluttered up with a vest.)

I did go back, of course, and at some point had my home-made tunic like the others – the first of many, for I danced with Jean Denning and Miss Ellen for years to come.

The repetition never grew stale, for every time was the same only different, the same only more so. The compulsion to dance flowered out of the class, and into other areas of my life, just as surely as there were times when the flow was reversed.

One such time still stands out in my memory. The heat of the summer's day became oppressive, the sky suddenly darkened, and the thunder and lightening were awesome. After it had passed there was stillness, broken suddenly by torrential rain. I stood by the window saying, "I wish I was out there dancing in it….." and Mother said, "Quick, then, it won't last long …… take your clothes off first." I was out in a flash. The rain hit my bare body in sharp stinging stabs, coming at me from every side as I ran and skipped, jumped and twirled and kicked up fountains. Only the tips of the grass showed above the lake of rain-pelted water, and soon I could feel the rain penetrate my hair and trickle all over my head until it flowed down my back and plastered my face with streaming hair. I tipped my head back, swept the hair away from my face, shut my eyes, and opened my mouth to see if I could catch a drink (I couldn't). And then the rain stopped, the lake was still and receding fast, and I tingled and glowed all over. It was the most exhilarating thing that had ever happened to me, and I treasure it still.

The next time we were told to 'be raindrops' in the dancing class I knew exactly what I was trying to recreate. Never mind 'drops' – I was dancing stair-rods.

In all those years no one day is as vivid as that first one, and I can't put an age, or even a chronological order, to the memories that follow – you can't dance stair-rods until you have experienced them, and there is no way of knowing when, or even if, this will happen.

But I do know that there was an overall pattern to the classes, and the variations came after the basics. We began with 'positions', and I remember the quietening-down as the class assembled, and we stood in rows with plenty of room round each of us.

Then it was, "*One* – heels together, toes pointing outwards – and *Two* - right foot forward towards the side; point your toes! And back ….." On we went to five, then we repeated it, without the reminders, "One! ….. and Two! …..and Three!" and then sometimes we repeated it without any reminders at all – the music told us by itself. It wasn't boring; it was lovely to feel the calm and balance that settled over us.

When we were hot and breathless came one of the trickiest (and most valuable) directives of all, "And *relax*….." This looked easy. You just lay on the floor on your back, arms by your side, and eyes shut. But doing absolutely nothing, not even looking, proved to be almost impossible for a long time – it must have been some years.

I rather think that in our younger days we were just told to, "Lie still, shut your eyes, and listen to the music," for when I first remember precisely how difficult it was, the setting was not The Hut. Whenever it was, I remember Miss Denning moving among us, lifting an arm or a leg, and letting it go again so that it flopped on the floor. I always saw her coming from under my eyelashes and, ever helpful, lifted up my arm or leg to meet her. She would shake it saying, "Let it go floppy," but I couldn't and she let go and, still helpful, I put it down again.

57

In dancing, as in life, the art of being able to relax at will is invaluable in restoring the balance of mind and body.

Once I had acquired it, the art never left me. I can still relax, and even drop off to sleep, wherever and whenever I want, waking refreshed after just five or ten minutes.

When we were ready to start again sometimes we heard, "Wake up in your own time, and when you are ready get up and do what the music tells you." In a relaxed state this was no problem at all. Sometimes it was, "Run to me," and then, "Now turn round and fly off like birds, anywhere you like."

At first I expect I just did what everybody else did – extended both my arms like wings, and 'flew off'. Over the next few years it slowly dawned on me that I could be my own bird – I could be a seagull, with my wings held steady as I floated this way and that. I could flutter and dart like a sparrow; I could shoot up into the sky like a small feathered rocket, before I just hung there singing; I could heave myself off the water, or the grass round the duck pond. I could be a Rhode Island Red Chicken, making a great flap and fuss, before flying a short distance in an untidy bundle of feathers.

Sometime we were told to walk like a bird, and I could be a hopping bird, a running bird, a run-and-stop run-and-stop bird, or I could be Grandma's cockerel with his stalking-strut.

The wonderful thing was that the background music would suddenly become personal as Miss Ellen recognised one of our birds, and joined us – you couldn't miss the trill of notes as you tried to leap up into the sky, or the lift, stretch, plonk of the cockerel's yellow legs and claws. We all loved being-like in our own way, and no one ever said, "Alice, would you like to show the others how to be a duck?"

We explored people: "Move as though you are happy... sad... cross... you are carrying heavy shopping... you have lost something ...

you are very old… " Was I going to be plump, smiley Grandma Gunary, or thin, silent, austere Grandma Bird?

I knew exactly how each grandma walked and stood and got up and sat down – but it was when I tried to make my face look like their very different faces that I began to feel what it might be like to *be* them. Being inside Grandma Bird felt sad and lonely, but being inside Grandma Gunary felt warm, and cuddly, and lovely.

Occasionally both teacher and pianist would confer over the piano while we relaxed. There were murmurings, and light snatches of music, and then suddenly both would burst into life at exactly the same moment. We sat up as the dancer spun off, watching in amazement, inspired and uplifted – so this was what dancing could be like! I longed to be able to move over the floor and through the air in exactly the same way. We clamoured for more, and Miss Denning would say, "I know! Let's all make up a dance together… " And phrase by phrase she would work something out, and we would follow her. By the end of the lesson we could put the phrases together, and dance a real dance – we, too, could 'do a Jean Denning', all over the floor and through the air!

We learned mime, with very precise hand movements so that we could say', "A tall man, with a beard and top hat, met a pretty lady in a bonnet and shawl, and arm in arm they went for a walk." And then we all made up our own stories.

We learned how to fall safely, and gracefully. I can feel and hear it now, "… and *run*… and *leap*… and *poise*… and FALL!" It is as fluid and easy as it sounds, once you learn to let go and relax into a controlled crumple. Soon the control element goes and it becomes instinctive. It is a lovely thing to do (with or without the fall bit) at low tide, on firm warm sand, after everyone has wended their way back to high tea and the beach is deserted.

Suddenly, I was 14 (school leaving age in those days) and Miss Denning told Mother she would like to have me as a student – how did she feel about it? Mother passed this information on to me, and asked how I felt about it. We were in the dining room by the fire, and that moment, too, is etched in my memory.

My heat leapt up at the thought of doing what I most wanted to do, all day and every day, not just for one hour a week. Money wasn't even mentioned; it was just an idea to be explored.

I decided I didn't want to do it, for a rather unexpected reason. It somehow seemed indulgent to drop all the school subjects that I didn't enjoy, in order to do something that I found so effortless and delightful.

On looking back I don't regret my decision, but I feel a little sad that I was tempted to opt out of school because it was such an uphill struggle and so unrewarding – and I didn't even know it wasn't my fault!

It isn't self-indulgent to discover what we love doing, and where our natural talents lie – that has been my aim for every child and adult that I have ever worked with. I want them to discover just how much they *can* do, and how happy they can be from *within themselves*.

If children (and adults) grow accustomed to being assessed by others, and by 'the system', they can come to accept that evaluation of themselves as true – and often it is not, or only partially so at best. The many and varied gifts they *do* have may be undiscovered, and wither away through lack of hope, recognition and use.

Both our children tried dancing classes at around four or five. Our son seemed to enjoy it. He plunged and pranced and plodded, most diligently – but rhythm eluded him, and as soon as he said he didn't want to do it any more we stopped.

But that isn't quite the end of the story. His inner happiness did express itself in movement in other ways, whilst endearingly recognising his physical limitations. He dashed in from the farm one day to tell me about a splendid escapade he had had, saying, "….. and I spriggered up, and squadded off!" And I thought, "He's got it!"

Our daughter, too, had her opportunity. But, "One … and two … and three … and point those toes," was never going to be her cup of tea. Even if she endured this and got to the, "And run on your toes … now skip!" part, it still seemed unlikely that it could compare with rounding up the cows in gumboots. We had to be fair, but as soon as she said she didn't want to go any more, we stopped it at once. There was no, "Just continue to the end of the term," because getting our money's worth wasn't what it was all about. We had wanted to offer her a joyful experience and it simply wasn't joyful. Enough said.

I wish that every child could at least be offered the kind of dancing to music that gave me so much pleasure. The essence of it is to help children to discover a source of happiness within themselves, and the means of expressing it, and of enjoying it alone as well as with others.

I speak with feeling for those children who also find that a spoonful of sugar – even if for only one hour a week – helps the educational medicine go down for the rest of the week.

Pets, living and dying

The first time we were given responsibility for something alive was when Grandfather gave us a pair of pigeons in a kind of pottery nest. He bred and trained racing pigeons. He also had beautiful white fan-tailed pigeons, but the ones we had were just ordinary ones. We took them home and installed them in a large wire-fronted cage, mounted on the sawn-off stump of a lilac tree to keep them safe from cats.

I didn't much like them, and certainly didn't want to touch them. They were newly fledged and although their feathers did cover them, the original yellowish down still poked through, making them look mouldy. We dutifully fed, cleaned and watered them and watched them grow with amazing speed – and then one awful morning I went out to see them and found one dead in its bowl.

I screamed and screamed, with feelings I had never had before. I was familiar with dead flies, butterflies, featherless nestlings, mice and voles, and also the larger birds – long dead and partly decayed – that we found on our walks, but this was different. This was bigger and it was *our* pigeon and all had been well the night before and now it was dead – and the deadness frightened and revolted me.

Mother came to the rescue and said that these things happened and it wasn't our fault because we had looked after them beautifully. She fetched a cardboard shoebox, put the pigeon in and said we would bury him in a nice grave. I remember asking if we could put flowers in the box, so we did, and the flowers made everything feel much better – I could put the lid on with a feeling of comfort and satisfaction.

Mother dug a surprisingly large hole in the herbaceous border, at the back near the hedge, and I put the box in feeling quite comfortable, but then there was a hiccup: I didn't want the earth to fall on the lid. So more flowers were called for, which made it all right.

We buried many other animals and birds, but this first experience was profound for me and the ritual was important. In retrospect it was fortunate that I didn't much like the pigeon, because that meant that I was introduced to death and funerals without the anguish of personal loss.

The next pet I remember was a small black rabbit bought in Romford market. I wanted to carry it home even though we were travelling the one station by train for a treat. We arrived on the platform together with a crowd of shoppers and their baskets, and I remember saying, "I shall call her Wendy because we bought her on a Wednesday," and suddenly I wasn't holding her any longer. She had jumped out of my arms and was hoping off among the legs and baskets, with me in hot pursuit, calling her newly-bestowed name. It took a while for people to begin to register what was happening, but then they all began to help, and eventually she was caught and handed back to me. Somehow I never much enjoyed my rabbit; she grew up so fast, and her back legs with their long, strong paws dug into me, and it wasn't a satisfactory cuddle at all.

And then came our guinea pigs. Pauline's was white with pink eyes and mine was ginger with brown eyes, and we loved them with all our hearts. They were perfect for cuddling; two cupped hands could hold their warm, firm, silky little bodies against our chest or cheeks, or settle them into our laps for a stroke, or put them facing each other at opposite ends of an apple peel and watch them munch like a couple of little steam trains till their noses met.

They also had another very important function, as confidants and comforters. Pauline and I were best friends — except when we hated one another, and pinched and scratched and pulled hair! When that happened, each of us dashed for our guinea pig and stomped off by ourselves, with our warm little comforters tucked under our chins or against our cheeks as we told them exactly what had happened, what was so beastly and unfair, and what we would like to do to each other. I am not sure that we would have put our honest thoughts and feelings into words if we hadn't been talking to a guinea pig as to a trusted friend. Mumbling to ourselves on the swing wouldn't have been the same. As it was, we held nothing back — and we didn't hear a single squeak of disapproval.

The guinea pigs came on holiday with us, in their open-topped wooden apple box complete with sawdust and dandelion leaves. One journey stands out vividly: we had a half-way picnic at the side of a field, and we let the guinea pigs out to have a drink and stretch their legs like us. They were very tame and we were completely unprepared for mine to shoot off and disappear down a rabbit-hole. Pauline grabbed hers and put him back in the box, firmly shut in the car, and I was frantic with worry that mine would be lost forever and we would have to go off and leave him to his fate.

On occasions like this, Father always came up trumps. He said, "We'll just sit here and wait for him," and Mother said, "He may find a nice furry family of rabbits in their burrow," a half-truth that took away some of the fear at the thought of him being lost and lonely in the dark all by himself. Mercifully, he reappeared just as suddenly as he had disappeared and we set off again, shaken but complete.

This was one of many experiences through which I learned that pendulums always swing the same distance each way: if you love greatly you also have the capacity to suffer greatly — you can't just enjoy the nice bit and expect to escape the nasty bit. It is one of life's hardest lessons to learn, and it starts long before school – especially if our parents will hold us steady as we try to cope with the aftermath, practically and emotionally.

One isolated incident involving animals stays with me. I remember going down the road one day and meeting a horse-drawn dray heavily loaded with sacks of coal. The horse's hooves were slipping on the surface as he strained to pull the weight up a slight incline, while the coal man sat on his seat above the horse, lashing out with his whip and shouting. Anger took hold of me, and I shouted that the horse was doing his best, and told the man to stop hitting him and shouting at him. I was completely unprepared for him to turn and lash out at me. I heard the crack of the leather thong and saw it snake out towards me – and I turned and ran for home as fast as I could.

You don't have to be dyslexic to know how you feel when you haven't exactly covered yourself with glory – you go over and over the experience in your head, altering it slightly here and there, until you really feel quite satisfied with the way you acquitted yourself! So it was on this occasion. When father came home I was ready and able to regale him with the saga in glorious Technicolor: the cruelty to the horse; my bravery, the coal man's attempts to whip me too – the lot!

If I had expected him to commend me, I was gravely mistaken. His response was short and to the point: "Don't be daft. He was no more trying to thrash you than he was trying to thrash the horse – it's the crack of the whip that gets the response." How true! With three women in the house all being loving, kind and sensitive, he was exactly what we all needed to restore the balance.

One day Pauline and I, aged about 14 and 11, went down to the piggery end of the farm and hung over a low wall watching a huge sow basking in the sun in front of her farrowing pen as she suckled a large littler of piglets. One little chap wasn't strong enough to fight his way in to find a tit and a space of his own, so he squealed and ran up and down the long line of suckling piglets, to no avail. Uncle Harry (the family pig expert) came along with Bob the pig man, took in the scene at a glance and said, "The littl'un will have to go. Knock 'im on the head."

We were appalled and said he couldn't do that. Uncle Harry said, "The sow hasn't got enough tits for a litter this size. The runt won't get enough food and will slowly starve – and as he gets weaker, the bigger ones will trample him underfoot."

Having hand-fed calves, we still couldn't accept this and told him he ought to hand-rear this one, to which the answer was, "We haven't got enough time," so we rushed in and said, "We'll do it." Uncle Harry said, "Take him with you if you want to," so we put him in a strawberry basket and took him back to the farmhouse – where we duly reared him on a bottle.

We installed him in a stout willow peck basket in the scullery, and in no time at all he had outgrown it and needed a bushel basket. Piglet housetrained himself with no trouble at all. He was as friendly and obedient as Mother's beautiful Labrador bitch and they were great friends, going everywhere together. Mother would walk round the garden with the pair of them in tow. If she gardened, they sat on the path and watched her. If Piglet got on the border to be nearer to her, all she had to do was say, "No, Piglet! Go and sit down with Candy," and he did. The three of us were exceedingly fond of Piglet – and father still hadn't said a word.

All was more or less all right, but Piglet's size began to pose problems and one autumn evening, crisis point was reached. The fire was lit in the evening and on this occasion Mother was in her armchair by the hearth, Pauline and I were in our smaller tub chairs between the fire and the pushed-back table and Father's chair was waiting for him on the other side of the hearth. Candy and Piglet came in, as they did for a while each evening, but instead of sitting on their haunches beside us, they elected to flop down full length on the hearthrug, covering it completely.

We three women registered simultaneously that the situation had become impossible, just as Father walked in. He stood there surveying the scene then turned on his heel to walk out as Mother said, "Ern, Piglet will have to go." He turned back, both animals heaved themselves up and went out into the kitchen at a single command, and he sat down.

This was a crisis on several levels. Piglet really did "have to go," which meant only one thing. He had to be sold to Dunmore Flitch bacon factory. We needed time to face up to this, but we hadn't got it because immediate action was called for. Mother said, "I'll install him in the shed under the walnut tree tomorrow morning. Is that all right?" and Father said, "Yes."

This was a pattern we knew, and all was now well at the family level. Father never forbade Mother to do anything because he trusted her good sense to know when enough was enough, and he knew that at that point she would turn to him for consultation – as a matter of courtesy, not subservience.

On the day the lorry arrived to collect Piglet, Pauline and I were cowards: we took ourselves off well out of earshot, knowing that Piglet wouldn't be abandoned to his fate. And so it was. The two men were amazed to see Mother and a pet pig walking down the garden path and, as so often happens, they responded appropriately. There was no shouting, no pushing, no grabbing – they just stood quietly by as Piglet trotted up the ramp.

We all felt awful, but it was infinitely worse the next day when there was a shout of, "Anybody at home?" at the back door, and a man walked in with a long open box, which he dumped on the kitchen table. It was the offal – in other words, Piglet's clean blanched trotters and head (split in two), his heart, liver, kidneys and tongue.

That was the most shocking and painful example of the 'discipline of consequence' that I ever remember in the whole of my life. Father had seen the van and followed the man to deal with the paperwork. We were still rooted to the spot in horror and he said, "You women *will* interfere with nature – what do you expect?" and left us to get on with it (quite rightly – if we are not confronted quickly with the consequences of our actions, how are we ever to learn to think before we act?).

I don't remember where Pauline was, but Mother and I had no alternative but to cope with the situation we had brought upon ourselves. There were no fridges in those days and offal had to be dealt with immediately, so we just got on with it: trotters in a large pan of water to render down for gelatine; both cheeks marinated ready to make brawn next day; tongue salted and simmered till tender before being put in a basin with a plate and weights to be pressed; kidneys washed, skinned and halved to remove the core; liver sliced to fry with the kidneys, together with smoked bacon from the last pig. I can't think either of us wanted mixed grill for our mid-day dinner, but Mother wouldn't have denied Father a meal he loved – and which we would all have enjoyed if we hadn't turned Piglet into a pet.

Learning to do jobs

At the top of a list of my ten favourite words would be 'jobs'.

Even now the word fills me with feelings of warmth and satisfaction, going back to my own childhood, and on to my children and grandchildren. The connections are clear to this day: Mother saying, "I've just got a couple of jobs to do before we go;" Father saying, "We should be able to start the job tomorrow, if the weather holds;" me saying, "Can I have another job to do?"

Move on a generation, and our own family is sitting round the breakfast table, as the four of us discuss what we are all going to do this Saturday. My husband says, "I've got a job to do on the car" (and when it's finished he will stand up, wiping his oily hands, saying with satisfaction, "Right, that's another job jobbed!") Our son says, "I'm going to work on my car. Ma, there's one job I need help with. Would you come and put your foot on the accelerator, and press it down when I say?" Our daughter says, "I'm going to play in Smelly Bonds," by which she means she is going to the large local store, to wander round the perfume department, being sprayed with samples – then she will come home and clean out her guinea pig. I say, "I've a few jobs to do in the house, and then I'll be out to play in the garden."

On to the third generation, with our son and daughter-in-law arriving for the day, and saying without fail long before they go, "Got any jobs you want done?" Our son is an engineer, and never goes anywhere without a few plumbing tools and his multi-purpose tool kit.

Then came the fourth generation, and our seven-year-old

grandson was staying alone with us for the first time. On the first morning Grandfather said, "Would you like to help set the table for breakfast?" to which the perfectly civil answer was, "No." We both boggled a bit, and had a good think. Then my husband said, "He gave an honest answer to a silly question. I'm going to try something different tomorrow." Come the day, "George, your job is to set breakfast," and he did it with alacrity, efficiency and the utmost good cheer.

Our granddaughter, at about the same age, showed her grasp of the word 'job' when she presented me with a jar of pickled onions for Christmas. I asked her if she had done them herself, and she said, "Well, I did all the jobs except peel the onions. Mummy did that – but I stood beside her and cried." I love her for knowing that not every part of every job is enjoyable, but as far as you possibly can, you stay with the job until it is done. I still think of her every time I buy a jar of pickled onions.

For four generations of our family, 'jobs' have been a way of life – not drudgery, or chores, just part and parcel of the process of living, to be taken in our stride as an essential part of family life. Above all, to be done *well*, lest carelessness in one part jeopardise the whole job.

I vividly recall the first time I did a real job. I had been aware that 'doing the fire' was one of the first jobs to be done each morning, but had never taken much notice. Then, for reasons unknown, one morning I suddenly 'saw' what was going on, and was absolutely riveted by the whole process. I sat in the armchair by the fireplace and watched intently, every day for days on end. I didn't say anything, or ask anything. It was a long, logical sequence of events, executed rhythmically and meticulously. Why had I never noticed before? It wasn't just a 'job'; it was a series of jobs, each following on from the one before. You started with a depressing, messy fireplace, and you finished with a sparkling hearth and a well-laid fire, waiting only for a match to bring it to life. How very satisfactory!

Then came the day when I woke early, and with the certainty that I knew how to do this splendid job – and I wanted to do it as a surprise before anyone woke up. Downstairs I went, and started to put it all into practice. I didn't forget a thing. So why didn't it go according to plan?

I fetched the Housemaid's Box, with the space underneath for the ash and the tray on top holding the brush, shovel, and strip of floor covering. It bumped against my legs, and the doorposts, but I got there.

I unrolled the floor covering and put it over the hearthrug, but I left a gap between the rug and the hearth and ash trickled through. I raked the poker through the dead fire, and all the ash fell through, according to plan, leaving the cinders on top of the grate. I shovelled up the ash, transferring it very carefully to the Housemaid's Box, but my wrist wouldn't turn properly and half the ash fell into the box, and the rest went everywhere in a great cloud.

I brushed round the hearth again, but the same thing happened. I put the cinders to one side of the hearth, and they felt horrid on my fingertips, not like anything I had ever touched before. The grate was so heavy I couldn't lift it out, so I had to drag it, and it left scrape marks on the tiles that wouldn't wash off. I carried out the box with the ash, leaving a trail behind me, through the hall, and the kitchen, and the scullery, past the coal-hole, and outside, where I tipped it on the pile by the dustbin – and it went all over my bedroom slippers, which I shouldn't have been wearing anyway.

The scrumpled newspaper bit went well, and I wasn't to know that the daily newspaper shouldn't have been confused with The Farmer's Weekly – which had to stay by Father's chair until the new one came. Making a wigwam with the firewood went well, too, but the cinders wouldn't stay where they were put.

I went into the scullery and fetched a stool to reach the tap, drew off half a pail of water, collected the floor cloth and sploshed my way back to the hearth. But even wiping the tiles wasn't as easy as it looked – too wet, and dribbles went everywhere; too dry, and smears spoiled the lovely shiny tiles.

My happy anticipation was wearing thin. In fact I felt very near to tears – why had it all gone so wrong, when I *knew* how to do it? I can't remember what happened next. I just remember the disappointment and despair that I felt, kneeling there surveying the scene.

This was to be my pattern for learning from then on. Watching, time after time, after time; rehearsing it in my mind (usually in bed at night) until I was absolutely clear about every detail, then waiting for the moment that said "Now!" before I tried it out – only to discover, yet again, the gap between doing it in my head, and doing it for real.

As a child I knew that I hated to be asked if I would 'help' with this or that. I knew immediately that it was a con. They could do it perfectly well without me. On the other hand, if someone called out, "Quick! Can you get a bucket and towel? The bath has over-flowed," then off I dashed to save the day, feeling useful and needed. Doing a complete job was where the satisfaction lay – or in joining a team as a fully-fledged member of that team for a genuinely joint effort.

I learned about children's need to do a complete job, not only from my own memories, but also from my son. He was three and a half at the time and suddenly he burst in upon me saying, "Come and see what I've done!" The urgency and excitement were unmistakeable.

I went where he led and suddenly, with a flourish of his arm, he said, "*There!*" I can't remember where we were, or what he had done or made. I only remember the radiant quality of his pride and joy as he added, "I did it all by my clever self!" What a lovely moment of self-knowledge for him. He had done a job of his own devising, in his own way, and lo and behold, it was good. And he knew it. He didn't need ratification from anyone – but he just thought it would be nice to share his moment of triumph with someone.

At moments like this we are called upon only to share the job and triumph – we don't have to add a thing. No, it wouldn't it be 'even better' if we put a flag on it! We should never seek to 'improve' a child's own unaided effort, unless we are invited to do so. If his own effort isn't good enough, why should he bother again? Why not leave it to clever old us?

Children need to learn to do jobs; they really do. If my pattern of learning is as universal as I think it is, how else are they going to learn about the gap that exists between what they *think* they can do, and what they actually *can* do?

I remember a reinforcement of this lesson when I was about 14 and suddenly wanted to move on from watching ploughing to doing it myself.

I had watched it, on and off, literally for years. Two glorious chestnut horses, side by side, pulled the plough between them: one walked on the hard ground waiting to be ploughed, the other walked in the furrow between that and the soft ground that had just been ploughed, with the plough slicing its way behind and between them. At the end came Cootie, just holding the beautiful curved wooden handles, walking in the rut between ploughed and unploughed, and at each headland issuing a sound of command as the horses turned and made the return journey.

On one particularly perfect day, sunny and warm, with soft, damp earth, I suddenly felt ready to try this beautifully straightforward job. I waited until after 'levenses'. As Cootie stood up, wiped his moustache on the back of his hand after finishing his bottle of cold tea, and removed Gilbert's nose bag, I said, "Can I try?" Cootie twinkled, and stepped back to let me step in his place – and less than a minute later I knew that I had been ploughing-in-my-head. I couldn't get my hands round the slender curved handles; they were huge. Cootie steadied the plough while I tried to find a grip; then he transferred the weight slowly, but I couldn't hold the plough upright. In all the time I had watched him, there had been no indication that weight was involved. Might a sense of weight be one of the latest to develop?

I struggled to stand upright for a few seconds, and Cootie didn't say a thing – he just twinkled even more than usual, then took the plough back, and set off on his travels again. This time I followed and watched with new eyes, especially as he issued the words of command (I could never understand what they were) to turn the horses at the headland: to turn two huge horses, and a wood and steel plough, so accurately that the new furrow fell on the one before with perfect accuracy, was skill of a very high order. The horses, too, became the focus of attention: their eight feet stopped, side-stepped and changed direction in perfect unison.

Grandfather's words of wisdom became real – he used to say, "Everyone in the world is better than you at something". Cootie certainly was, and I have never forgotten it.

One of the reasons for recalling my earliest memories these last three years has been to see if I could detect any signs that I was already dyslexic. Were there any problems that other people shared with me, or was I already 'different'?

With this in mind I phoned my farming cousin Dennis, who had been a friend since childhood, to compare our memories of farming procedures. We are the same age, and he is by no means dyslexic, yet our memories of this gap between perception and reality are the same. He remembers his first serious ploughing at about the age of fifteen, and his gaps were my gaps.

In his head he thought the horses plodded along slowly all day. In reality, when he grasped the plough the horses set off at what felt like 40 miles per hour. In his head, he thought the ploughman just held the handles of the plough, and plodded slowly behind the horses. In reality, the newly ploughed furrow was narrow and rough to walk in, the plough was heavy and had to be held in balance, and he seemed to be scrambling, plunging and staggering along with no rhythm at all.

In his head, the horses just turned round at the headland, as the horseman called out what sounded like, "Wock Malla" (turn to the left) and, "Cobby Ware" (turn to the right). In reality, although the horses responded to the words, he was required to do more than hold on if the plough and horses were to turn accurately before re-tracing their steps.

In his head, he didn't think much about the plough at all, beyond knowing that the iron ploughshare that made the first cut into the ground wore out quite frequently, and had to be repaired. The steel breast was protected by the iron ploughshare, and cut through the earth throwing the soil in an undulating wave to one side. In reality, the depth of the furrow was his to decide, with all due circumstances taken into consideration. At his first effort he ploughed down into the ground to what felt like a foot, and the horseman shouted at him that he would break the plough. At his second attempt the plough was whizzing along the surface, not doing any work at all.

We agreed that this gap was probably true of all of us. But if so, it poses certain problems. What if children aren't given the opportunity to watch a wide variety of people working? What if, every time something, or someone, catches their eye and they long to stand and watch, we don't give them that time?

What if, having not taken in what a job requires, they get it all wrong and are told off? Do they persevere, or do they eventually give up trying?

Worse still, do they kid themselves they could do it, without ever putting themselves to the test? Is this why we have so many 'wannabees' with a desire to be successful whilst having no realistic sense of their own abilities?

CHAPTER 3

Spontaneous play
(i) Outside

Mud pies

My sister and I were in complete agreement, as we looked back to our childhood, that if we had been allowed only one kind of play in the garden it would have had to be mud pies. There is nothing quite like mud pies!

One of the corner stones of our play in the garden was a heavy circular rustic table. It had been 'made to last' by Grandfather, who built his farm carts on the same principle. It was the perfect height for us when we stood and used the top as our work surface – as we did for our mud pies.

We started by tipping small buckets of earth on the top, then we scooped a hole in the centre and poured water in, rather carefully – it held the water to our great satisfaction. After that we stirred it with sticks, still rather cautiously, until the earth from the sides of the hole began to crumble into the water. The more we stirred, the more earth fell into the centre, until the pool became mud and had drawn into itself the last of the buckets of earth.

We had no measure for how much water to how much earth; we tipped and mixed and progressed from there. It is in retrospect, after watching countless children over the years, that I recognise how much our apparently random mixing, and theirs, may have been borrowed from adults. We sometimes mixed in the same way as Mother making the Yorkshire pudding, with the light folding-in of the flour to join the eggs and milk in the hollow in the middle; on other occasions we mixed it as Father made cement, which meant using the garden trowel or an old kitchen palette knife to slap the outside edge of the heap into the hole – not just once or twice but again and again, very firmly, followed by short, sharp downward cutting movements. I can't think we ever said, "Let's do it the Yorkshire pudding way," or, "Let's do it like cement mixing," and we certainly wouldn't have registered at that stage that one method was designed to trap air in the mixture and the other to expel air, but I am inclined to think that we copied these two methods – whether we knew it or not – from watching both jobs being done so many times.

In any case, does it matter? I rather think it does, for without a pattern to copy we could probably have sploshed on by trial and error, but we would have missed out on the beautiful rhythm and precision of the adult movements. I know that rhythm and precision in movement have always been a source of great pleasure to me, and I know too how dependent I am on visual imagery in my learning.

Sometimes we added too much water, which then offered two choices: we could poke about under the privet hedge with golden syrup tins to find dust-dry earth to add to the too-wet mixture; or we could add more water until we had mud slosh.

The first solution had one drawback: the dust was full of dead leaves, and sometimes spiders, which we didn't much like. However, it was essential if we wanted mud we could mould with our hands. The second solution ruled out making pies, but instead we could 'paint' the table, including the legs, with house-painting brushes, and watch it dry in pale streaks.

Each type of play had its attractions – and the painting exercise gave our play an extension, in that we had to wash it all off if we wanted to eat in the garden. However, if this operation happened too close to dinnertime, we discovered, the table was uncomfortably wet and not too clean. We soon learned!

As our play evolved, we relied more and more on memory recall and personal experience. We made 'dinners', with hand-moulded chicken or joints of meat or chops; we scooped out mud dishes and filled them with pale coloured stones for boiled potatoes, or brown stones for roast potatoes, and torn-up leaves for cabbage. We improvised plates from large laurel leaves and when the 'food' was carved and served, a generous helping of thick mud 'gravy' was poured over everything.

'Party teas' were another favourite, with leaf sandwiches, and cakes decorated with flowers. I am glad we had seen, eaten and helped to make the real things, for they were so satisfying to reproduce.

We did try our hand at making mud plates, but that didn't work, though I did make a small teapot, about the size of a large walnut. I remember taking it into the kitchen to ask if it could go in the oven to be baked hard. I can't think I knew about the firing of clay pots, and can only assume I was remembering the slices of stale bread being slow-baked to hardness ready to make breadcrumbs. Anyway, it worked. The lid didn't come off and it wouldn't pour, but miraculously the handle remained intact. It is the first thing I remember making, and I was so proud of it. I fetched my Reeves paint box and carefully painted it a beautiful cobalt blue, then I mixed red and yellow and painted an orange band round its middle. Then it looked even more beautiful, and I kept it in my bedroom for years.

Our garden shed

At the end of our garden was a small shed, which housed the lawn mower and garden tools. There came a day when Mother said she thought we children needed the shed more than they did, and at the weekend we all trooped out into the garden, and Operation Clear-out began. It was the kind of job we greatly enjoyed doing together, each according to our skills and strength.

When the shed was empty of everything but cobwebs, spiders and dust, then division of labour became marked: Mother removed the spiders and cobwebs and said we could use the soft broom, dustpan and brush from indoors to start cleaning. Father found alternative places for his bits and pieces and Mother stood by to consult and help.

My sister and I flourished brooms and brushes with much enthusiasm, and a clear idea of how one went about such tasks. The air was thick with dust, and we sneezed and spluttered, but the floor began to look splendid and we felt we had really taken possession of our prized property – it wouldn't have meant nearly as much to us if someone had 'done it' for a surprise.

The scrubbing was the best bit, and we took it in turns to fetch endless half-full pails of clean water, or to be the one who scrubbed. The soap wouldn't lather at first; the boards were so dry they absorbed the water too quickly. But gradually they became wet enough to produce a grey scum, and the floor cloth became grey and slimy – and the plants nearest the hut had copious drinks of filthy water,

My sister's heart murmur meant that she grew tired long before I did, and she went indoors or sat and watched Father. My energy was inexhaustible, and I fetched, carried, scrubbed and watered the plants until meals or bedtime stopped me.

The scrubbing went on for days, and each time the floor grew lighter in colour and the soap suds became pale, and the lather followed the sweep of the brush – east and west in smooth lines following the grain of the boards; north and south against the grain, needing two hands and yielding no pattern of bubbles – but best of all big figure-of-eight sweeps leaving lovely scrawls and loops of bubbles. I *loved* scrubbing!

We used vinegar and water for the single large window pane, and a nail brush for the framework timber that gave us a continuous ledge round the hut about chest high – we used it as a kind of mantelpiece. We had a small collapsible table (that everlastingly nipped our fingers) with two small matching armchairs, given to us by a generous relative, and Mother found us a small cupboard with two shelves and a door with a brass knob.

Curtains were next on the list, and making them was easy. We just cut in half a cheap sale remnant, paid for out of our pocket money, and hey presto, we had a pair of curtains ready to sew. I don't remember if I made a hem at the bottom and sides, but I do remember making a hem at the top because we worked out that we would have to put a stick, or piece of string, through it to hang them up. But how? The window frame was made of pieces of timber rather like the 'mantelpiece' strip, much stouter to bang nails into than the boards. We found the hammer, and two long nails, and I knocked them into the frame at the edge of the window. So far, so good.

But how to get a piece of string through the hem? We had watched knicker elastic being threaded through by attaching a safety pin to one end, and wiggling it through the hem – but a safety pin wouldn't attach itself to string.

At this point we had to give in and ask for help. Mother suggested a piece of tape – but by the time the safety pin was in the tape it was all too fat to go through my narrow hem. There was nothing for it but to undo the hem and make a bigger one. I hated undoing anything I had done, but even more I hated things not to 'work' – and asking someone else to do it for me was worst of all. This pattern of learning stayed with me for years, and there were many times when I grew cross and tearful, but eventually, when I felt ready, I usually went back to it because the finished job was so clear in my mind that I couldn't bear not to make it happen.

When the tape was safely through the new hem, there came the gratifying moment of anchoring one end firmly round one nail, and stretching it across the window to anchor it to the other nail. Triumph! Except it wasn't. The cheap fabric was full of 'dress' to give it a substance it didn't really have – and instead of pulling back to each side of the windowpane in graceful folds, the material stayed stiffly along the tape to exclude the light and view of the garden. The sharpness of the disappointment stays with me still. But the open door let in the light, and we still loved the material.

We never ceased to enjoy putting our 'house' in order. We looked through old plant and seed catalogues, or seed packets themselves, and cut them out to make pictures for the walls. We stuck them on the walls with flour and water paste, and then we improved upon the plan by mounting them on stiff wallpaper from out-of-date wallpaper books. Or we mounted them on cardboard, and then they were stiff enough to prop up on our 'mantelpiece'.

We started a collection of small glass pots to use as vases – the most satisfactory were Shipham's paste jars. They were perfect for the mantelpiece and table and we were always free to pick marigolds, pansies and nasturtiums.

The hut began to look like a home, and we put books, paper, pencils and crayons in the cupboard for rainy days – that was when the hut really came into its own! We would scuttle down the garden, and sit there in state, watching the rain and feeling somehow special. It was like being on our summer holidays in a small fishing village on the Norfolk coast – there was never a holiday when we didn't have to retire from the beach and squash into our patched and faded canvas – covered hut, with the wet bathing costumes and towels hanging from string washing-lines.

I can't explain how we felt, but we knew we shared it – we could fight like cat and dog from time to time, but *never* in the shed. We never took our dolls in there to play at Mothers and Fathers, for the simple reason that we didn't feel like parents when were in there. Neither did we feel like our parents' children. We just felt like *us*: responsible home owners, self-sufficient and self-contained. Calm, wise, capable of deciding when we could venture out – or dash into our parents' house for hunks of bread and two spoons to take back to *our* house to eat with the small jars of homemade jam we made indoors under mother's eye and stored in our cupboard.

The more I recall our childhood, the more grateful I am that we were thrown back on our own devices to create play opportunities for ourselves. We were offered opportunities, such as an emptied garden shed or old packing cases, but we made our own way from there – and the more we did it, the more our imaginations worked from what we *had* to what we *might* have. And whatever we made, we became more attached to it as we worked – step by step, job by job, result by result.

Young children's perception is fuelled by their achievements, not by money. They don't crave perfection as we see it; they love what they have made themselves, no matter how amateur it may look to us. Our adult part in this is to spot opportunities to leave 'props' lying around for them to discover – and to allow them 'watching time' so that they can stock the storehouses of their minds with visual images and experiences that can be drawn upon later when their imagination is sparked by need.

Converting our shed into our home, we drew heavily on years of memories of what you did to make a house into a home. We had done for ourselves, after a fashion, every single job that made up the creation of our 'home'.

Miniature farms

Our miniature farms were an endless delight, displayed on our bedroom windowsill in winter and spread out on a patch of lawn in the summer – if we started after the weekend mowing, they could stay in place for the whole week.

We started with the farmhouse, a Lyons Swiss Roll box covered by stuck-on paper, on which we had painstakingly painted, drawn or crayoned small bricks – sometimes further embellished by Grandma's wisteria over the front, and her ivy all over one end. But before the ends were covered we had to insert some large stones, otherwise the slightest wind blew our 'farmhouse' away.

The roof was a sheet of corrugated cardboard, folded in half, and stuck on with glue – it looked like reed thatching with its brown ridges running from top to bottom. Other small boxes made the stables, cow shed, chicken house, pig-sties and barns – or we made these extra buildings from our wooden building bricks, only then the farmhouse and the farm animals were disproportionately small.

We marked out the fields with twig hedges, or a fence improvised by turning big cotton reels on their sides and threading a hollow wheat straw through the holes. The fence was a bit low but we were happy with our token fences until such time as we thought of something better.

At last we were ready for the shoebox! This contained our most precious possession – our collection of farm animals. Our pocket money matched our ages, and went up by one penny every birthday.

Spending it presented no problems at this stage in our lives – we each wanted two gob stoppers, and two liquorice boot laces, which accounted for one penny each, and all the rest of our money was spent on farm animals.

The ritual was definitely part of the pleasure. Wednesday was Romford market day, and off we went on the top of an open-topped bus – heavy woven willow baskets or light flat plaited 'fish bags' in hand. First came the queues in Sainsbury's for butter, bacon, sausages and cheese; then the hardware shop, or chemist, or drapers, or Woolworth's, according to the needs of the week; then the market stalls for fruit and vegetables we didn't grow on the farm – and *then* the toy shop. At last! Mother stood or sat at the back of the shop, surrounded by shopping bags, and we were free to spend as long as we liked in front of the farm animals shelf. They were lined up in parallel rows, from the front of the shelf to the back, according to size and price; all perfectly moulded and cast in lead, all perfect in colour and detail.

I seem to remember that baby chicks were four for a penny, and hens and cockerels perhaps two pence each. There were sheep and horned rams, and lambs on spindly, wobbly legs – but our absolute favourite was a creamy-fawn ewe, sitting, with her little white lamb snuggled into her side. There were black and white Friesian cows, brown shorthorns, dainty little Jersey cows, sitting or standing, or heavy bulls, or long-legged calves. Horses came in carthorse size, or ponies for pulling traps or milk floats, or for riding, and Shetland ponies. Boars, sows and piglets came in black, black and creamish white, or cream all over, and the piglets matched their mothers.

After the animals came the extras: dog kennels with dogs that fitted inside; a chicken coop (another favourite) for broody hens, with a slatted front that opened up, so that you could put the nesting box with the sitting hen right inside – then you spread corn just outside so that she could put her head through to eat when we weren't looking; hurdles that never stood up properly unless they were hooked together as square pens; milking stools and pails; long low troughs for water, circular troughs for pigswill, large free-standing water troughs for cattle in the field; wheel barrows; farm workers in mid-stride with hand clenched round a circular hole that held the handles of a wheel barrow or the shafts of a plough.

At the end of all these delights came the wishful thinking, unattainable, daydreaming section – you didn't even contemplate ownership, because you knew it was absolutely out of the question. And yet, one day after a distressing, frightening and painful session at the dentist, the unthinkable happened – Mother said, "I think you have earned a treat. Let's go to the toyshop for something special!"

So off we went, and I was led to the place where prized pieces cost half-a-crown (just over 12p now). I chose the horse-drawn hay rake, with a mechanism for lifting the long line of curved prongs so that the hay could be released before being lowered to rake up the next load. This time the ploughman walked between the horse and the rake so that he could operate the lifting mechanism. This magnificent present gave us untold hours of joy.

Our collection was so precious to us that we never left them out overnight. I don't think we thought in terms of them being stolen, or carried off by dogs wanting to take a present back to their owners – it was just the feeling that if you had something you valued, you had to be responsible for its safety and well being. I don't think children have to be dyslexic to invest valued possessions with human feelings – and if you know you wouldn't want to be locked out of the house at night, you certainly wouldn't want treasured possessions to be subjected to such treatment. Although it was time saving and convenient to leave the farm setting in the garden overnight, it was a bonus having to set the animals out each morning – for that was the climax of our enjoyment.

At time went by, we added the all-important extras to bring further realism to our farming. We put rice grains in the chickens' nesting boxes for eggs, and we scattered crushed Force (the early version of cornflakes) as chicken food. Chocolate drops were the cowpats we dotted about the pasture, and currants the sheep droppings – but I do remember that where imagination and reality met head-on, it was not as easy as we might have imagined to eat the chocolate drops and the currants when we packed everything away for the night.

In the same way that we drew on our family home life to create our own 'home' in the shed, so we drew upon life on the family farm to create our own miniature farms. Again and again we drew on reality, and on our involvement with real jobs in the real world.

Since discovering I am dyslexic, I realise how little I have been able to learn from books – and how dependent I have always been on watching, followed by doing. And how lucky we were to have so many hours of uninterrupted watching time, and immersion in the real world, throughout our childhood.

Imaginative play

For most of the time Pauline and I played together in complete harmony. I had unlimited energy of mind and body, ideas were never in short supply and I never needed to use her to fetch and carry; I enjoyed saying, "I know!" and dashing off myself to get whatever it was.

Pauline's heart murmur made her less physically active. Her role was to be there as happy and willing passenger. The upturned kitchen table on the lawn was our life boat and we were the only survivors of a shipwreck. I would dash off for a broom and some dusters, give the broom to Pauline and say, "Hold it against the table leg and I'll tie it firm with the dusters." Pauline dutifully held it and our mast was erected. Then I would decide we needed a sail, so off I beetled and came back with a sheet from the dirty clothes basket and together we fixed it to the broom – more or less – and then it was time for a flag, so off I would go for a tea towel.

Meanwhile Pauline would scour the horizon with imaginary binoculars and announce that she couldn't see another ship – or that she could, "Over there!" – and we would both stand up and wave in vain.

Then we sat still for a bit and tried to catch fish. After that we decided we were hungry, so off I shot to ask for some dry bread – "hunks, not slices," and sultanas and a salad cream jar full of milk. Returning, I did the doling-out-of-rations bit.

Where Pauline came into her own was in padding out the story lines. Mother read to us both by the hour, and we could both join in

when it was a long-established favourite such as *Wind in the Willows,
Winnie the Pooh* or *Alice in Wonderland*. But Mother and Pauline quickly
outstripped me and they went on to enjoy much longer books of
adventure founded on fact, such as *Swiss Family Robinson, Robin Hood
and* (surprisingly early, on looking back) historical novels about Sir
Francis Drake, Sir Walter Raleigh and Queen Elizabeth I. One snippet
I do remember we enjoyed acting out – a dashing sailor and adventurer,
kneeling in front of Queen Elizabeth saying, "Your Majesty, I have
brought you a potato," and her reaching out and saying, "Good gracious
me! Whatever is that? We'll have it for dinner." Children have a happy
knack of reducing things down to *their* bare essentials.

As farming children, we could relate to tales of adventurers who
brought back potatoes, tobacco and the seeds of new flowers and trees.
We were also familiar through our annual summer holiday with a small
Norfolk fishing village, so we could appreciate stories involving tides,
storms, red flags, cliff falls, flat calm seas and trawlers landing a variety
of fish. When we tried to catch fish, Pauline knew about whales that
tried to overturn our raft, or giant squid that would reach horrible
suckers over the side of our life boat to try to tip us over – we had to
bash them with our oars or axes, and as fast as we freed ourselves from
one arm, another would appear.

We found no difficulty in suspending these very real adventures
for the time it took to snap back to reality in order to grab a sheet or
provisions from the house and board our ship again.

How lucky we were to have so few toys, radio limited to
Children's Hour, no television and no computer games in those early
years! We can't halt 'progress', but I warm to the parents who suddenly
realised their children never played with each other. They banned TV,
radio, videos and the computer during weekdays and rationed them at
weekends – "and for the first time the boys played with one another."

Picnics

Picnics are a way of life in our family — not a cheap or convenient substitute for a 'proper meal'.

The essence of a picnic for children is food eaten in an unexpected place and way — the more unorthodox the better. Under trees, up trees, in a field, in the back garden, in the front garden, on a balcony, under a dining room or kitchen table, on a beach, squashed in a damp canvas beach hut with rain pelting on the roof, in a car, on a train, eaten from a communal basket or from individual bags or packages. (But a packed lunch isn't at all the same thing as a picnic!)

First generation

One impromptu picnic stays with me. It was a lovely sunny afternoon, and the suggestion was, "Let's go and pick blackberries, and take some sandwiches with us." So off we went to a field near the station where large blackberry bushes were dotted about. We carried a walking stick for pulling down fruit-laden branches, a selection of small baskets, and one larger basket containing the picnic. We picked until our baskets were full, and then sat down to eat our jam sandwiches. I remember one of mine was stained red where the bread was too thin and the jam too generous. We also each had a Heinz Salad Cream jar of milk. All was going well, when Mother suddenly said, "Pack everything up — we'll finish our picnic in the garden." It was the tone of voice to be obeyed — no panic but definitely a sense of urgency. We were on our way in no time, and when we reached the stile out of the field I looked back, and saw a man appearing round our bush on his bottom by means of stretching out both legs, digging his heels in, and hitching forward. If I had known the word 'furtive' it would have flashed into my head. As it was I knew I was frightened, and that was enough. As he saw us depart he got up, fawn raincoat trailing, cap pulled down over his face, and ran off in the opposite direction.

I never again wanted to go in that particular field, and I can still see that particular red stain on that particular sandwich.

Second generation

Because every family cycle is different, but compelling in its own way, my sister and I passed our love of picnics on to our children — we repeated the kinds we knew, and added new ones of our own.

I remember one winter when our son and daughter were seven and four, they caught measles from one another, followed by whooping cough. Having been wisely and well looked after in our own childhood, nursing them came naturally, but even so, it was an anxious time — though much easier than coping with convalescence!

Once they were up they were whiny and grumpy, with short attention spans. Nothing entertained them for long except being read to — and I read until I was hoarse, and my eyes kept closing. Then picnics came into their own, and most of the children's interest centred round the staircase. They chose which step they each wanted for their picnics every day, and their interest held until each child had tried every step.

When it came to invalid cooking, all I had to do was to forget the steamed fish and parsley sauce of our childhood, and substitute sandwiches with Marmite for one child and banana for the other, hard-boiled eggs, small fingers or squares of cheese (preferably mixed colours) or triangles of cheese in silver paper, small potatoes in their jackets filled with mashed potato and butter and sprinkled with cheese, and small Heinz tomato ketchup bottles of milk with a straw.

Sometimes none of these things worked, and it was back to basics with plain bread and butter sandwiches, white or brown, or one slice of each colour.

I remember how their interest even held to include pretending the stairs were a double-decker bus. One would be the passenger and decide whether to travel on the top deck or the lower deck, and the other would be the conductor – only instead of issuing tickets he or she would issue an item of food.

Third generation

By the time picnics had reached the third generation, I remember a particularly nostalgic one. I went to stay with our grandchildren, when they too were about four and seven, and I took a toss-in cake with me. At tea-time, by prior arrangement with my daughter-in-law, the children and I went up to the end of the garden under the old apple tree, carrying the cake, a bottle of milk, mugs and a knife – and the magic words, "Mum says you can eat as much as you like!" And they did, more and more, slower and slower, until they found they had to say, "I can't eat any more." And that was part of the satisfaction – for how can you know what is 'enough' until you have found the limit for yourself?

I am glad they weren't sick because it would have spoiled things for them – but I was also very proud of them, and of their parents for having graded the choices offered to them over the years until they had come to know for themselves how much is 'enough'.

Spontaneous play
(ii) Inside

Dressing up

In a corner of our bedroom there was a large, heavy wooden packing case, stamped *J. Carter and Co* in thick black letters – it belonged to an era when goods were sent abroad by ship, and containers had to be strong enough to be loaded onto horse-drawn wagons, bundled off at the quay, swung up by cranes, and dumped in the hold of the ship. I don't know exactly how we came by this prized possession, but there it was in all its ginger varnished glory, discreetly hidden under a rose-covered curtain with a dark green border.

It held all our dressing-up clothes, and gave us hours and years of pleasure. I know it was full, but certain favourite items stand out. There was a short, white georgette evening dress of Mother's, dating from about 1918 – it was gorgeous, with pointed 'handkerchiefs' of material hanging down from a dropped waist to flutter in peaks below the hem, and on the shoulder was a floppy chrysanthemum made of the same material.

There was another evening dress, which had started life as pale coffee lace, to be worn many times before being dyed chestnut brown. Some time later it was given a new lease of life by the addition of a crisp cream organdie ruffle, which made the skirt swirl beautifully. Later still it was dyed black, and when it came home from the cleaners and dyers I vividly remember Mother bursting into tears and saying, "I *can't* wear it any more times – I just can't!" And she didn't. She gave it to us, but we never liked it much. The horrid colour, and the memory of the upset, stayed with us, and the associations were always rather sad.

Another favourite was a waistcoat of Father's with a shiny back, and different front, with buttons all the way down. There were also his old plus fours, which made splendid, long baggy trousers, with braces that hitched them up under our arms.

There were scarves, and shawls, and bangles, and curtain rings on wool loops to hang over our ears. There were pyjama jackets (the trousers having worn out), and a huge, pale mauve woollen bed jacket, knitted by Mother, that had stretched and drooped until it would have fitted an elephant. There were the best bits cut from sun-damaged curtains, some blue and silky, some heavy brown velvet.

And hats! One of our favourites was a straw hat with a wide elastic band round it, into which we could stick feathers, flowers, cherries, leaves or anything else that caught our fancy. There were wonderful fat tea cosies, which the Aunts made for each other at Christmas – one had sides made of rich crimson satin, ruched just so, and worn with a velvet cloak. We nearly burst with importance.

And finally, there was The Fox. We definitely didn't like it, and could hardly bring ourselves to touch it, and yet we couldn't be parted from it. There was the hard, vicious little head – we had seen what a fox could do in Grandma's chicken run – complete with bright glass eyes, and the beautiful tail at the other end. If we held one end each, the four legs dangled down in a floppy kind of way. Ugh! It was backed with soft brown silk, and had a beautiful link chain and a hook and eye fastening, covered in silky braid of some kind. You had to be brave to put it on, draped over one shoulder and clasped under the other arm, but after a minute or two something extraordinary happened – it felt as though you were wearing a hot water bottle! You couldn't look at, let alone touch, the dangling legs, but in spite of all this it bestowed upon us a certain 'feeling' that nothing else quite did.

Although I remember walking up and down the landing, and parading in front of the long mirror on the wardrobe door, I don't remember playing a whole game in which we acted out our characters. What I do remember is that each garment gave us a special 'feel' – and that was what we enjoyed.

We didn't possess, or need, any 'outfits' to be a nurse, or fireman, or shop keeper, or parent – we knew what they *did,* so if we *did* what they did, then we would know what they felt like while they were doing it, wouldn't we? Simple! We had real models for all these roles. The shop keeper, Mr Wallace, bustled, and bowed, and beamed; Mrs Collett laughed and waddled under the weight of her wonderful pile of dark, shiny coils of hair, and all her cauliflowers were "beautiful;" Mr Burr held nails in his mouth, and spat them out as required as he hammered new soles on Father's shoes and boots.

We knew very little about what kings, queens, princes, princesses, lord mayors and such-like *did*. We gleaned a bit more from books Mother read to us – fairy stories were full of them – but there was a gap between our imagination and our ability to *be* them. We fell back on dressing up to try to give us a 'feel' of the importance these people obviously had.

Sorting and grading

The pantry

My sister and I loved those days when it was time to give the pantry a good spring clean, and enthusiastically offered our help. The first step was to clear the shelves and put all the jars, tins, packets and bottles on the newspaper-covered kitchen table – that was *our* job.

Meanwhile, Mother scrubbed the lowest brick and tiled shelf, followed by the wooden shelves above. We always knew how far she had got because a scrubbing brush on tiles sounds quite different from the same brush on wood.

I remember that where the gravy-browning bottle had stood there was a dark brown stain and one day I suddenly realized why. The golden rule was that we could borrow anything we liked, as long as we asked permission first and put it back exactly where we found it – and gravy browning was something we borrowed in order to turn flour and water white 'icing' for our mud pies into 'chocolate' icing. We duly asked, borrowed and returned the bottle but nothing was said about washing away the dribbles, so we didn't. Eventually, I made the connection between a messy bottle and stained shelves.

The shelves had to be left to dry, but then came the best bit, when we could return the items on the table to the clean shelves. This was when the fun began. How should we do it? Tallest things at the right hand end and everything graded down from there to small jars of Shipham's sardine and tomato paste at the other end? Or all the bottles at one end, then the glass jam jars, then the tins and lastly the bags and packets? If we did it that way, it still felt right and proper that within each group the correct height order should be maintained.

Eventually it dawned on us that the pleasing sight of contents arranged just so wasn't the only consideration. When it came to helping on baking days, we found ourselves in difficulties, scurrying up and down the shelves hunting for ingredients that used to be kept next to each other for convenience. We were allowed to return to our re-arranging on those days when all else failed to inspire us. When we were played out, Mother took over and without a wholesale re-grouping of everything, over the next few days and weeks, she gradually restored her chosen order as she removed ingredients for use and then replaced them elsewhere.

The button box

Four generations of Mother's family added to the button box and the contents ranged from large bone buttons off the caped coat worn by Grandfather when he took to the road in his first open car, to tiny pink and blue buttons off all the babies' first kid shoes.

My sister and I played with this treasure trove just as our mother had done before us and our children did after us and all the time the collection grew. Pauline and I dipped our hands in and tried to stir the buttons – an odd feeling, cool and smooth, with ripples running through our fingers; then we lifted handfuls and let them trickle out on to a large tray; then we ran the palms of our hands over them and swirled them around. (30 years later, our children did exactly the same things, with no prompting or example from us.)

Then we looked at the buttons individually and began to sort them into as many different groups as we could devise. If we sorted by colour, red, blue, yellow and green were simple. But then we were left with greeny-blue, grey-green and mauvy-blue. Whichever pile we put them into, they looked wrong, so they had to go into a pile on their own. That led to a new game. One of us chose a colour, say red, and we took it in turns to find and name as many different reds as we could: scarlet, crimson, beetroot, magenta, puce, flame, cerise... Whoever found the last name started us off again on a new colour. Love of colour and love of words overlapped and both were important to us.

We had other categories for sorting: those we liked and those we didn't; the biggest and the smallest.

I inherited the button box and our son found his own focus of attention. He went briefly through the size and colour groupings; then the metal, wood, bone, mother of pearl, glass and plastic groups; then he focussed on his greatest interest – the number of holes – and finally reached a classification that defeated me. I could see no linking connection, such was the diversity of colour, size, shape and material, so I asked him. And back came the answer: "These haven't got any holes on top. You have to sew them on through a little sideways hole sticking out at the back." He was three and a half at the time. He had discovered the button box as I sat by the fire sewing for the baby and he sat beside me on the floor sewing buttons onto blanket pieces. He became an engineer and I realise on looking back that his interest in sorting, construction, assembly and workability was always present in everything he did so methodically. Self-chosen play is hugely important, as long as we just allow it to happen and develop, without making any assumptions as we watch.

By contrast, our daughter's interest in the button box was exhausted in about ten minutes! There is no accounting for taste, and differences within families are profound.

Life styles change, but I have been interested to see that family patterns like ours still persist, even if in a different form. Children are given the cutlery tray to sort, or the laundry basket; or the plastic bags full of shopping are left on the kitchen floor, whilst children un-pack them and have time to do some sorting of their own before put-away time; or a load of cardboard boxes from various shops are provided, ranging from big enough to climb in to small enough to fit inside each other.

There are plenty of sorting and grading toys in shops, in brightly coloured plastic or wood, but children prefer reality. Education is for living and if these practical observations are made in the context of daily life, they provide an invaluable opportunity to link play and work.

Experiments

Given the opportunity, I think most children would go through the stage of wanting to find out by experimenting – and quite often they would use the same words to describe what they were doing.

Mixtures

I can remember a particular day when I was in the pantry with an empty jam jar and a teaspoon. I was going along the shelves putting a teaspoon of everything into the jar and stirring it vigorously. In went marmalade, raspberry jam with all its pips, strawberry jam with its lumpy little strawberries, cocoa powder, coffee, tea leaves, salt, pepper, vinegar, salad cream, white sugar, brown sugar, flour, milk, chicken bone stock, currants, sultanas, raisins – and then gravy browning, which spoiled everything. Up to that point, everything I added had altered the colour slightly, or the texture, or the smell, but the gravy browning obliterated everything else.

Mother came in, saying in friendly fashion, "What are you doing?" and I said, "Making mixtures." She replied, "I used to do that when I was a little girl." I loved those moments of bonding.

Many years later I found our eight-year-old son going along the shelves in the cupboard under the stairs in the small semi-detached house we were renting at the time. I asked him the same question and he gave me exactly the same answer. He was older than I had been, but then I realised that when we were living at the farm, the shelves had been too high for him to reach.

When our daughter was four, she discovered the same fascinating experiment and described it in exactly the same words: "I'm making mixtures."

No-one who remembered how fascinating this had been to them in their childhood, surely, could find it in their hearts to be cross about mess or waste? It was all done so seriously and deliberately, with close inspection, sniffing and cautious tasting at each addition. The mess occurred between scooping-out from the original container and tipping it into the mixture: wrists wobbled, liquids came out too fast, the spoon knocked on the rim of the mixture jar or the spoon was heaped too high, but none of it was caused by carelessness. What happened after each addition was carefully scrutinised – we really did want to see 'what would happen if …..'

And why not? We had watched our parents and grandparents cook, and adding, stirring and tasting was an inevitable part of it. If we hope our children will enjoy cooking for and with their families, then the more interest they show in the component parts of the operation, the better.

Scents

Scent in my generation was named after the flowers from which it was made, such as rose, gardenia, jasmine, violets and lily of the valley. We duly sniffed the small bottles and cakes of soap, then went into the garden in search of the original so that they could be compared. If we were lucky enough to be hunting for something that was in bloom at the time, that was a great bit of good luck. And, yes, lavender water or cologne did smell exactly like the lavender in the garden. So we went ahead and tried – without much success – to make our own.

For us, the names of the flowers evoked the perfumes, but

107

advertising and marketing created different links for later generations. I remember our daughter working on Boots perfume counter one Christmas and coming home very pleased with herself. An endearing customer had wanted to buy perfume for her granddaughter but could only say, "I don't know the name, but it's the one where the air hostess walks down the gangway of the aeroplane." Luckily, the advertisement rang a bell and the gift was duly bought and wrapped.

Stains and dyes

We learned very early on that tea spilled on a white tablecloth stained, and so did the juice of beetroot or blackcurrants. So what more natural than to try out other liquids to see if they did the same thing?

My sister and I cut pieces off a gauze bandage and stuffed them into everything we could find: stewed rhubarb, custard, tomato ketchup, gravy, coffee and Bovril. We also tried rubbing some pieces over tins of brown and black shoe polish, and immersing them in mud. Then came the testing bit: we took the pieces upstairs and put them in the bath with us. Some came clean and some didn't – fascinating at every stage!

I remembered these experiments years later when I did weaving, spinning and vegetable dying for my major project in the second year of craft finals at Bedford Froebel Training College. Boiled onion skins and various lichens from the Hebrides were a revelation. As in childhood, there was no way of telling in advance which bark, leaves or roots would yield a dye, let alone what colour it would be.

I remembered something else too. I wanted to work a fine sampler of the first 25 years of my life and I searched in vain for a really fine piece of natural-coloured linen. And suddenly the store-cupboard of my mind gave me the answer. I bought a wonderfully fine white linen baby's pillow case, unpicked it, washed it, made a large pot of medium-strong tea, strained it through a handkerchief and immersed the fabric in it until the depth of colour was right. The sampler hangs over my bureau still. The silks have faded, but not the tea-dyed background.

The more I think about it, the more sure I become that if only more children were allowed the freedom to learn by 'doing', and given the time to repeat and improve on what they found out for themselves, then those who later proved to be dyslexic at school would be less damaged by the shock of finding out that they were 'different from' and 'not as good as' others. They would already *know* that there were many other things that they loved doing, and could do well – and they could go on adding to their mental filing system as they continued learning more and more outside school and as much as they could inside school.

Needlework

I remember sewing from a very early age. Mostly it was centred on my dolls – which I loved and treated as though they were my children.

Not all little girls loved dolls as I did. (My sister grew up loving her ever-growing family of personalised stuffed animals.) For those of us who did, it provided a focus for other skills. Initially, we picked up other skills just because they looked interesting, such as sewing – but we found a ready use for the things we made.

The earliest stitching I can remember was with a crewel needle, short and stout with a rounded point and a large eye. The snag was that the thread had to be tied to the eye of the needle 'for safety' and the knot prevented the needle from pulling the thread smoothly through the material.

I hated and resented it more than I can say, to the point where I decided I didn't even want to try any more, and at that point a compromise was found. I still had to have my wool or thick embroidery cotton tied to the needle, but was given special canvas with large holes that allowed the knot to slip through more easily. What I wanted to do, which was to pick up one or two stitches at a time on the needle before I pulled, still didn't happen – but I greatly enjoyed the 'stab' stitching, pushing the needle down to the other side, pulling the thread after it and then stabbing it up to the front again.

Eventually, every clock, vase of flowers and ornament had its own mat to stand on. What is the point of making something with pride and joy, if no one wants to use it and enjoy the result?

Another craze was for sewing on buttons. By this time, I had graduated to a proper needle – with proper cotton cut long and doubled, and a knot to join the ends. Scraps from a homemade dressing gown took the needle and cotton beautifully. The buttons of assorted sizes and colours looked splendid dotted all over the needle-cases which then became the next Christmas presents.

Because family history tends to repeat itself, I still have – and use – two such needle cases made from the same button box, by our son nearly fifty years ago.

Then came *real* knitting – small squares to be joined together to make dolls' cot and pram covers and kettle holders, and Pauline made an orange tie which Father nobly wore when he and Mother set off for a dinner dance.

Dropped stitches were a disaster at first and all attempts to rescue the loop that kept dropping further and further down only made matters worse – until I discovered that if I had a big nappy pin beside me, I could catch the errant loop and hold it safely while I dashed for help. As long as I could keep thinking of ideas to rectify whatever it was, I didn't panic or despair.

In fact, having ideas was very gratifying in itself. I still enjoy the feeling of, "I know – why don't I....?" and this is a reaction common to many children like me. We seldom, if ever, go to reference books. We just look inside our heads for relevant experiences or cast a 'seeing eye' on the problem before us, or talk to someone who is on our wavelength but several (or many) years ahead of us.

When I was about 7 or 8, my maternal grandmother died. We had a wonderful time looking through the contents of the attic, which had been assembled on the lawn. Among many fascinating objects, there were toys: dolls' prams with china handlebars; shuttlecocks and battledores; train sets, stilts, tops and whips.

Best of all though was a little sewing machine about 30cms high that actually sewed when you turned the handle and helped the material to run over the plate where the needle jabbed up and down. Because of my passion for dolls and making things, it was given to me. There followed years of experimenting and joy, and of problems to be solved that were exactly the kind of challenges I loved.

I had watched Mother cut out and make our dresses using a one-piece brown paper pattern handed down from Grandma and I knew exactly what I had to do. The paper pattern was much too big for any of my dolls but I reasoned it would work just the same if I folded the material in half and laid the dress that I wanted to copy on the material – shoulder seam along the fold. This I did, cutting out a scoop for the head. Then all I had to do was join the side seams together – turn it inside out and, lo and behold – a dress!

But, it didn't quite work out like that. The finished dress wouldn't go over the head or around the doll's arms. I tried again (and again), making the sleeves wider each time and the hole for the head bigger. Eventually, the dress went on, but the neck gaped hugely. Not only did it look unsatisfactory, but I knew the doll would be chilly around the neck.

But what to do? The first solution was to run a line of stitching round the neck, put the dress on, then gather up the thread until it fitted snugly, then fasten it off securely. Then the doll looked warm, comfortable and attractive. But I couldn't take it off without cutting the gathering thread. I grew tired of following this procedure every time and had to think of other solutions. It suddenly occurred to me to look through our own dresses to see how they were made. Some had buttons and buttonholes along both shoulders. Some had a slit down the back fastened with a button or press-stud. I tried both methods, but the back slit seemed best as I couldn't manage the buttonholes. Then I found the material frayed round the press-stud. Back to our dresses again and I discovered the strengthening device called a 'placket', but I couldn't manage that either. Then I had another idea. What about a slit down the front, so that it went on like a coat and didn't go over the head at all? That remained my favourite solution for a long time, finished off with a belt or sash.

My first major undertaking was a petit-point evening bag. I saw the offer in a women's magazine and the full-sized illustration grabbed me. I wanted it and I had to have it *now*! I didn't even think about its usefulness or otherwise. I wanted to touch it; to work on it with needles full of glorious colours – honey, coral, lime, turquoise and the soft neutral background. I wanted in particular to work on the petals of the central flower. They were long, swelled in the middle, then tapered to a point and one had a fascinating twist to it, as though the wind had ruffled that one petal.

Mother helped me fill in the form; took me to the Post Office and bought a postal order and off it went. Back came two pieces of fine canvas, stamped with the coloured guidelines, a bundle of embroidery wool that exactly matched each colour, and a gilt chain and clasp to finish it off.

I became obsessed. I took it up to bed to work by torchlight. I got up at first light and went downstairs to continue until breakfast. Every available minute found me stitching and it began to look beautiful. Eventually, the first side was finished and I started on the second. Then suddenly I had worked myself out completely. I couldn't do another stitch. I can remember the moment. I was sitting in Father's brown rexine armchair, having unpacked my needlework bag, and I just couldn't pick up the sewing.

Even if all the words I have at my disposal now had been available to me then, I doubt I would have been able to find the right one. Not 'guilt', because I had nothing to reproach myself with; not 'disappointment', because I was so devoid of feeling that there was no emotion; not 'anxiety' because there were never any recriminations if our energy or enthusiasm just came to an end; not 'dread' because we were never forced to finish anything as a discipline.

So what made this time so devastating? Perhaps because this time I had invested so much of myself, for so long, in the biggest sustained effort I had ever made, and I wasn't equal to the task.

I didn't want to go to Mother for comfort or explanation, let alone help. I just wanted the whole thing to go away. So I bundled it all up, canvas, wool, clasp and chain, and hid it I know not where. This was not the hiding of deceit, but of the desire for oblivion for my sake. I still don't remember where I hid it but it stayed untouched for years. When it eventually came to light, I was surprised to see how good it was – but had no desire to finish it.

Should Mother have tried to slow me down, to ration how much I did at a time? Should she have warned me at the beginning that it was too ambitious? Did she know about the torchlight sessions? Of course! Should she have put a stop to them? Should she have asked where it was, when it disappeared?

I don't think so. Children need time and repeated experience to discover their interests, abilities, limitations and (eventually) their pattern of learning. I knew from a very early age that I always wanted to tackle big jobs, to go for it, so that my whole self was stretched to the limit – and, sometimes, beyond. Father used to say, "Don't go all out again; it will only end in tears," and quite often it did. But it never stopped me from doing exactly the same thing the next time.

What is wrong with finding our own way of coping with feelings that build up inside us until they can no longer be contained? Frustration, temper and tears are as much a part of our make-up as laughter, excitement and tranquillity. I had just discovered another (temporary) solution – denial!

It's all part of the learning process and if we are controlled too tightly, we can give up and deny our creativity. Eventually we can begin to understand ourselves and achieve a better balance.

Cooking

I learned to cook by watching Mother and enjoying everything about those lovely cosy mornings. Pauline would be sitting in her high chair, drawn close to the table. I would be kneeling on a cushion on a dining-room chair that allowed my feet to stretch backwards. Mother would be standing between us. The kitchen boiler threw out glorious warmth, and the only sound to be heard was the occasional *clink* of Mother's wedding ring against the large yellow and white china bowl, as her hands dipped in and out making pastry. (That sound has stayed with me all my life.)

At first neither of us wanted to help. It was enough to be there enjoying the moment. Eventually, I wanted to join in, helping here and there, sifting the flour; adding pinches of salt; dropping in small pieces of butter and lard from a teaspoon.

Then I learned to rub the fat into the flour. Mother made it look so easy. Her hands dipped into the bowl, came up high, her fingers rubbed together and down fell a gentle shower of crumbs. Easy! Can I try? But of course, there was more to it than met the eye. I repeated the movements but somehow the fat got squashed together with the flour and fell down in horrid lumps. I ended up, not with a bowl of crumbs, but with a bowl of hand-hot fatty blobs!

By the time water had been added, my blobs became a satisfying lump, ready to be rolled out, cut into circles and put in the bun tins. I loved using the tin cutters and I got sidetracked into making all sorts of shapes – no good for jam tarts, but they cooked beautifully on a flat baking tray. By this time Pauline was joining in – making shapes with her hands, slapping, pinching, rolling 'sausages' and generally doing whatever was possible without sharp tin cutters. When everything came out of the oven, Mother's tarts didn't look the same as ours and hers crumbled when you ate them. Ours were quite hard to bite, but they were '*ours*' and *we* claimed they were better. No one contradicted us. We just became more proficient as time went by.

We learned to prepare casseroles, Mother scraping the vegetables and cutting them into chunks, while we sifted the flour, a few pinches of salt and a sprinkling of pepper onto a plate. The pieces all had to be rolled in the flour before they were arranged in the casserole. But first, while the colours were bright, we played with them rather as we had with the button box. We put the colours in groups. We made same-colour rows, arranged lines in colour sequence and, of course, tasted as we went along. When we tired of this, we rolled them in the seasoned flour and packed them into the fat brown pot, whilst Mother browned the cubes of meat 'to seal in the goodness' and stirred them into the vegetables.

Later, we took on more tasks by ourselves. A toss-in cake was one of the first things Pauline and I learned to make, and it took a whole morning to prepare.

We had heavy Avery scales with a stack of circular weights that all fitted into each other. The smallest ones were brass, and went from a quarter of an ounce to eight ounces, the etched numbers showing up clearly on the shiny surface. The heavier weights, from one pound to four pounds, were iron painted in a silver colour. These were very heavy to lift, and had the weights marked larger and in a different way.

We spread the weights out in a long row, and hunted for the eight-ounce one first, which we put on the scales, then we tipped flour into the scale pan until it balanced like a see-saw. This took ages because we took it very seriously, adding or taking away flour by the spoonful. The flour went into the big yellow and while bowl with a swoosh, and the weight went back into the line-up before we hunted for the four-ounce one, to be balanced by a much smaller pile of sugar. The same process was followed, and then we had to find the twelve-ounce weight for the mixed dried fruit. There wasn't one! I rather think we dashed off to the fount of all wisdom to say that it had been lost, and were probably told that there wasn't one, but we could put the four ounce weight on top of the eight ounce one, and together they would be perfect.

I don't remember when it was that we could confidently pick up two, or even three, weights together to give us the right amount, but I am absolutely sure that no real job was ever interrupted by information or questions that we didn't need at that moment.

Another serious bit of business was four ounces of margarine. We had no idea that half an eight-ounce block would do the trick, so we laboriously (but happily) kept adding bits cut off with a teaspoon until the scales see-sawed. At this point it was taken from us in a small saucepan to melt on the gas stove, while we progressed to the delightful instruction, 'two eggs, not beaten': one egg each; just the job! We cracked each one on the rim of the bowl, and sloshed it in. If broken shell went in too, it was easy to see and fish out with our fingers.

After this it was three eighths of a pint of milk, and a piece of sticky paper on the outside of the measuring jug told us when to stop pouring. Last of all came a pinch of salt (one each as our 'pinches' were small) and half a teaspoon of cream of tartar, and we knew exactly where that lived in the pantry.

And that was that, except for the beating and mixing by hand. We made a beeline for the eggs, stabbing the yoke with our fingers, and proceeding from there. We dug up the flour, let swirls of milk flow into the gaps, tried to find the sugar hidden under the fruit, and gradually saw all the individual ingredients become a lovely general mess. We dug and mixed until our fingers and wrists grew tired, and we were glad to hand over to a pair of adult hands, and watch it being beaten up until it was full of small bubbles – then the bowl was held over the cake tin (if it was lined it certainly wasn't done by us at that stage), and we scooped it out and helped it on its way, until the bowl was scraped clean (but not *too* clean, for licking out the bowl was the crowning glory of a job well done).

And then, years later – I must have been at least 14 – came one of those days when I woke up full of energy and enthusiasm. I said to myself, "I know – I'll have a cooking day," for no other reason than that I felt like it. Always one to seize the moment, I cleared it with Mother before she went out in the garden and I started. I don't remember what I made. I had no plans for these wonderful days that burst upon me every now and then. I just started and carried on. As soon as one thing went in the oven, I started making the next thing. And, when the first one came out, the next one went in – sometimes, yet another at the same time, but on a lower shelf. Oven temperature and baking tins and trays were 'juggled' as I went along. Somewhere along the line, a boiled 'spotted dick' was tied into its floured pudding cloth and put on the range to bubble away gently, ready to follow cold meat and pickles at one o'clock. And before it was time to put the cloth on the table, a large sultana cake went into the oven to cook slowly while we ate.

I can remember spreading all the cake racks along the big old dresser and every one was laden, probably with a chocolate Victoria sponge, biscuits, pastries, a treacle tart, cheese straws, rock buns or other favourites. There was also a bowl of butter icing to spread on the sponge when it was cold.

Dinner was on the table on time and suddenly I knew I was

absolutely burned out. Why did I never see it coming? The excitement of the moment kept me going, as idea followed idea. If we hadn't stopped to eat, I would probably have gone on even longer. (Eventually it became known in the family as 'going out too far'.) I felt triumphant, but suddenly I was aware of the fact that the draining boards, the end of the kitchen table and the top of the oven were piled with dirty tins, bowls, utensils, jugs, lemon squeezers and goodness knows what else – all waiting to be washed up!

The meal ended and with her usual empathy, Mother said, "Well now, you did all the cooking, so my contribution will be to do all the washing up. Off you go!" And off I went. I knew that the general rule was that if you made a mess, you cleared it up. I knew Mother must have been as tired as I was. I knew I was being let off lightly, and I was just *so* grateful. There are times when the exception to the rule is more valuable than the rule itself.

In time I grew quite brave with the kitchen range. You had to keep an eye on the fire and on the wind outside – blowing from one direction and the food burned on the outside and remained raw inside; blowing the other way and the fire wouldn't draw at all, so the food just sat there. I still couldn't read print intelligently but learned to 'read' the wind, the fire and the relationship between draughts, dampness and oven temperature.

This is learning that has to be done by 'feel' and experience. I have always had an insatiable appetite for learning, as long as it comes to me through a medium other than books, and as long as I can *learn* rather than being taught, and learn at my own speed. When there is something I need to know, I will ask. I am highly receptive, as long as I am told only as much as I need to learn at that point.

I think this is the pattern of learning for many children. It needs to be recognised and encouraged before school whilst learning is still a joy. If we lose confidence in our ability to learn, then things go from bad to worse.

The cycle moves on through the generations

Both of my grandchildren are sharing accommodation with four others of similar age and stage, and I asked them what arrangements they made about their evening meal. Both said the plan that had emerged was for one person to be responsible for one evening meal a week. I asked how well it worked. George (22) said, "Two of us can cook. One can't cook a thing but he wants to learn and is coming on quite well. It's the fourth one that is the problem. He fancies himself as a cook, with his speciality being sauces. They are indescribably awful!" Rachel (19) said she and one of the boys could cook but not the other two girls. "Not a boiled egg, poached egg, or fried egg. Not even a scrambled egg!"

Our son (56) said, "I can't remember a time when I couldn't cook." I asked if he remembered the 'cooking stool' we had made for his fourth birthday. It was about 45 centimetres square, with solid sides that sloped outwards, so it couldn't rock or topple – high enough for him to be at the right height to put two slices of bacon into the frying pan. We used to stand side by side watching the white bacon fat slowly becoming transparent and then colouring to golden. Then it was time to put the small cooking slice under the rashers to turn them over. We watched some more. The fat began to run out of the bacon into the pan. Then the cold mashed potato could be put into the fat and patted down, so that it too became brown and crispy underneath before being turned over to brown on the other side. Then came the eating!

Bacon and egg was a bit more tricky. Breaking an egg is something our children found quite difficult, even as we had before them. It demands so much concentration and there is a danger of wrists coming into contact with hot frying pans. Then we watched some more as the transparent egg white slowly became cloudy and then solid white.

Eventually, about three years later, he could cook a 'Pirate Feast' as a weekend treat: bacon, egg, sausage and fried potato. Either his father or I were in the background in the kitchen. Accidents can happen with hot pans and fat spitting near flames. We were prepared to act fast, but we saw no reason to put fears in the way of such a naturally careful, methodical child who was enjoying himself so much and so profitably.

We would have been much more cautious about our quick-silver daughter. Fortunately, she showed no early interest in cooking, although she loved making such things as yellow and red jelly rabbits on green chopped-up jelly grass, trifles and highly imaginative sandwiches. (Why did I think sardines mashed with strawberry jam might make her sick, when I would have been happy with sardines on toast, followed by strawberry jam on toast?).

It is giving me great pleasure and hope for the future to recall watching and cooking with five generations of women (and our son and his son), on both sides of the family.

Imaginary friends

Because of Pauline's heart murmur, we fell into a pattern of playing together whereby I instigated our play and did all the dashing about and she was happy to be included in a passive role. This worked well for several years (give or take the odd squabble), but there came a time when she had had enough of being taken for granted and staged a quiet rebellion.

We were playing 'Mothers and Children' in the dining room, where each of us had a home behind an armchair in the corners on either side of the fireplace. We endlessly dressed and undressed our dolls as we talked about what we were going to do and how we were attiring our children for the occasion. I don't remember us actually emerging from behind our chairs with dolls suitably clad and embarking on one of these outings; the planning seemed more important than the end result.

However, on this occasion, Pauline suddenly said she didn't want to play any more. We both emerged from behind our chairs and met on the hearthrug. I began to remonstrate with her and suddenly she took the wind right out of my sails. She made no effort to state her case but with great dignity said quietly, "Come on, Acki, let's go and play by ourselves," and she disappeared under the dining room table where she was hidden from view by the thick brown chenille table cloth with its plaited fringe which almost touched the floor.

I could hear quiet talking going on and eventually said humbly, "Can I come and play with you?" to which the answer was, "No. We are quite happy by ourselves." I was stopped in my tracks. There was absolutely no way I could defy those words and the quiet authority with which they were said.

Acki became a permanent member of our family. We took her seriously as Pauline's 'invisible friend' and, intuitively, none of us trespassed. We never attempted to evoke Acki for our own ends. Mother never said, "Acki says she's ready to go upstairs for her bath now," and even I never dared to say, "Acki says I can play with you today."

Pauline enlarged her family. I don't remember the arrival of Buddy and Tatty, but I was there when the last member arrived. Mother and our Aunty Ida had taken us to Ilford to have our photographs taken and when it was all over, we were taken to tea in a shop – our first experience of such grandeur. (Pauline was three and I was five and a half.)

We were led to a little table with a white cloth and someone in a brown dress with a cream apron and a matching headband brought us a silver tray with a silver teapot, milk jug and sugar bowl, and glasses of milk for us in silver holders with handles. We had toasted teacakes and then came a silver cake-stand covered in wonderful cakes. After this, there was ice cream in silver cups on stalks. Never was there such a feast.

When we had all finished, Pauline said "Can I go and kiss Borslaw?" Mother replied, "Yes," and we watched her slide off her chair and go in search of our kindly, comfortable and rather elderly waitress. When she found her, she put up her arms and said, "I want to kiss you," and Borslaw was quite overcome as she bent down to meet her.

I don't remember how long Pauline's family lived with us – one or two years at a guess. They didn't need to be fed, dressed or put to bed. They were just 'there'. I remember puzzling about the state of invisibility. Could I become invisible? If so, how? Could Pauline really see Acki, Buddy, Borslaw and Tatty? It certainly seemed so. She knew them so well and protected them against me at every turn. "You didn't hit her; she jumped out of the way." "She doesn't want a sherbet dab; she's just had her dinner."

There were times when we still played together, just as we always had, and on these occasions either the 'friends' were forgotten or they tagged along to the call, "Come on! We're going to make mud pies."

Sometimes they took centre stage, as when Pauline would say, "I can't go to bed yet. I've got to go and get Acki, Buddy, Borslaw and Tatty in from the garden," to which the only possible answer was, "All right – while you do that, we'll go on up and you come when you've brought them all in." It worked. It was a bargain, as invisible as the friends themselves: *You treat them as though they were real and I won't take advantage of you.*

And the message to me was, "You treat them as though they are real, or you will find yourself isolated while we withdraw and play by ourselves."

What I do remember vividly is the day they all departed. We were going on holiday. The car was packed and ready for off. Father settled himself in the driving seat, put his hands on the steering wheel and uttered the time-honoured words, "Right! Anyone forgotten anything?" Up piped Pauline, "We can't go yet. Acki isn't with us!"

She got out of the car, opened the garden gate and disappeared down the path leading to the back garden. Not a word was said, but Mother and Father shared a silent smiling glance and we all settled down to wait. I remember the turmoil inside me. What was I supposed to do? Should I offer to go and help in the search? Was Father going to get impatient and toot the horn? For once, I didn't have an answer, so I did nothing. Eventually Pauline reappeared, got into the car and said, "Acki's ready now." So off we went.

After that episode, Acki just faded away. It was as though this invisible presence had given Pauline the courage to make her own presence felt. Pauline and Acki together had been able to stand up to me and get their own way without any confrontation. Pauline and Acki together had been able to hold up the whole family, again without confrontation. She counted! She was an equal member of the family and knew it to her complete satisfaction. Buddy, Borslaw and Tatty also departed – no longer needed as extra 'back-up'.

Once, a year or two later, Acki re-appeared briefly, as true friends do in a crisis. Pauline had to go into hospital for a week and in those days, not even mothers could stand up to a matron in full sail. Parents had to leave the wards as Big Ben, just over the river, struck four o'clock each afternoon and were not allowed back until it struck 11 times next morning.

All went reasonably well during that first day. Pauline unpacked her personal things, chief among them Wilf, her long-eared blue rabbit with a white tummy and lining to his ears, and Ted in his black trousers, orange velvet jacket and bow tie on an elastic band around his neck. Then came her books that Mother was going to read to her every day. Then things began to get a bit edgy as it drew near to the time when Mother had to leave. Tears and panic threatened to overwhelm her. Suddenly, the day was saved. Pauline called out joyfully, "Acki's here! And she can stay until you come back tomorrow morning."

All was well.

After lights out

Grandfather Bird's house was full of clocks. There was a huge and sinister clock in the dark corner at the turn of the stairs – I hated and feared it beyond measure. I always shut my eyes as I passed it, sometimes on tiptoe so it wouldn't hear me, but at full pelt after dark in case it 'got me'. It wheezed its way to a full strike four times every hour – and when it struck one in the daytime, it was accompanied by Grandma's vigorous banging on the gong at the foot of the stairs.

The dining and sitting rooms had very large clocks on the marble mantelpieces, one under a glass dome, which I enjoyed looking at. When this clock chimed it was the clearest and loveliest sound imaginable.

The dining room clock was obviously related to the monster on the stairs – it stood on a heavy marble block, and there was a bronze horse rearing up, and a mounted soldier holding aloft a waving flag. He was clearly going to dash off and kill people.

The consequence of Mother having been brought up in this clock-dominated house was that we had no clocks at all – except the alarm clock by Father's side of the bed that went off at six o'clock every week-day morning, and Mother's tiny watch on a narrow black ribbon round her wrist. We really weren't aware of clock-time at all; we just knew that dinnertime was one o'clock, and Children's Hour was five o'clock, and bedtime was six o'clock. We had a hazy grasp of hours and minutes; an hour was a huge amount of time, so long that you didn't have to bother about it – and a minute was much, much shorter, but, "I won't be a minute" seemed a bit variable.

Every evening we were given notice that playtime was coming to an end. Usually it was, "Ten minutes before clearing-up time," which gave us time to draw to a conclusion whatever it was we were doing. But I have one vivid memory of a glorious summer evening, when Pauline and I were immersed in a particularly happy world of our own. We had created quite a lot of clearing-up, so the call was, "You've got 15 minutes more," and we both wailed, "No! Please, we're not ready, we're having such a lovely time," and back came the reply, "Well, suppose I say quarter of an hour?" And we were overjoyed and full of gratitude!

I wonder why I remember that episode so clearly. I know exactly where we were both standing, by the border under the hedge. I can't think I knew we had been conned, so it may have been the strong association I had between 'minutes' and anything to do with the word 'hour' seeming so much longer. And yet ….? There came a moment long after when this episode came back to me, and I *did* know it had been a con. But I also knew we hadn't been lied to, because I remember Mother's words so clearly.

Usually we were quite ready for bed, having worked and played ourselves out during the previous eleven hours, and anyway the bath time ritual was much enjoyed. There was no shortage of hot water, and no economy over the amount. No chilly duck puddle for us! The water came nearly up to our waists, and we sat one each end, with the wooden soap rack over the bath between us. We tried to change ends by sliding under the rack without touching it – or one would join the other in the big end. We took it in turns to slide down the slope with a whoosh, trying to make a tidal wave without it going over the top.

Pauline was always out first, and I had the bath to myself, rolling over, or holding myself up with my hands on the bottom. The sure-fire way to get me out was to pull the plug, for when the water got low enough it would start to swirl round the plug hole faster and faster: At that point I grew panicky, saying, "Get me out! Get me out! I shall go down the plug!"

Once in bed we snuggled down, were given a good-night kiss and heard the familiar refrain, "Goodnight, sleep tight, see you in morning." (The goodnight kiss was never withheld, no matter how trying we had been. Sometimes it was a bit chilly – nevertheless it was important.)

And then anything might happen! Sometimes we were so tired and fell asleep so quickly that there wasn't even time to enjoy the delightful sensation of falling asleep. If we were still awake when Father came up to see us, then another ritual took place. He would say, "What have you two been doing today?" and if it had been a lovely day, we would just say one word, "Playing!" But if it had been one of those days when everything jarred and went wrong, we summed it up in the one word, "Nothing."

Sometimes he would be so tired he just fell asleep beside us, and I can remember feeling that we were guarding and protecting him – we didn't move a muscle, until eventually Mother came up to find him.

When we were finally alone, we took it in turns to suggest what we should do next. Sometimes it was tapping tunes on our pillows, and the other would have to guess what it was. Usually it was a Nursery Rhyme, and as they had such a satisfactorily pronounced rhythm we didn't take long to recognise it, but if we didn't it would be tapped out again and again, with increasing emphasis, until we both began singing it in unison. The National Anthem was immediately recognisable, it was so heavy and plodding, "God Save Our Gray.....shush King."

We enjoyed inventing and describing banquets for each other, in which tinned sardines, cream slices and baked beans figured prominently. Both our Grandmas were wonderful cooks, so it wasn't difficult to go on and on, course after course.

Occasionally we planned a meal for our worst enemy, and this always featured boiled Savoy cabbage (with its leaves full of hateful raised veins which clung to our tongues); trifle with sherry in it; shiny, dark red jelly, absolutely ruined by the wine Grandma poured into it; boiled cod with a lot of black skin and no parsley sauce; and the skin of cold custard with stewed rhubarb – which set your teeth on edge with a unique grittiness that made it impossible to close your teeth together, because of the shivers it sent all over your face and neck.

We designed wonderful ball gowns for the grandest occasions. We could talk about what they would be made of as we knew quite a lot about the names and 'feels' of different fabrics, not only through helping to sort out the laundry basket on wash days, but also through Mother's annual purchase of a half-crown bundle of assorted scraps from Liberty's January Sale.

Sometimes we dived down to the bottom of the bed to make houses with our pillows and the feather bolster. This involved much heaving and pushing in a very small space – which eventually became so hot that we had to come up for air.

One of our favourite games was to release the covers at the foot of the bed, turn them down, and change our pillows from one end to the other – then we dived down from the top of the bed to the new 'top' and put our heads on the re-positioned pillows. The transformation of the view never ceased to amaze us – the curtains were on the wrong side of the room; so were the two chairs with our clothes folded in a hump ready for the morning; above all, the light and shadows on the walls and ceiling were different – instead of looking at the bright crack of light from the landing outlined by the door, we looked into a soft haze of light that was almost dark. We always tried to stay awake after this switch, wanting to see if our parents would be fooled into bending over to kiss our toes on their last look-in on their way to bed – but we never managed it.

We never played any of these games when we went to stay with our grandparents, partly because we never went together, or if we did, we didn't sleep together – but mostly because the two houses were *so* different that they elicited totally different responses.

Mother's family home was overpoweringly oppressive:, the rooms were too high, the Victorian mahogany furniture was too heavy and too dark, the long heavy lace curtains cut out the light, the corridors were too narrow, too long, and lit only by one small bulb of light – but above all it was brooded over by that sinister clock on the stairs.

I tried to stay alone there several times, sleeping with my greatly loved Aunt Ida – but it never worked. As soon as she had put me to bed and gone downstairs, the panic set in. The street lamp outside threw the shadows of the lace curtains on to the ceiling, and not even the reassurance of the passing cars could lift their threat from above my head. I didn't dare go to the top of the stairs to see if I could hear the comfort of voices – and creeping downstairs to listen outside the drawing-room door was impossible. The clock stood between me and safety, tick-tocking, wheezing and striking like a monster waiting to pounce.

Eventually Aunty would come up to see if I was asleep, and always found me weeping under the bedclothes. Nothing could pacify me, and eventually she had to phone my father and ask him to come and get me. Without fail he came, never cross, just gathering me up in a rug and tucking me into the front seat beside him – and immediately I felt safe, and all was well.

Father's family home was long and low, with sloping floors and wide floor boards, odd steps here and there, and beams in some of the walls and ceilings The furniture was old, faded and friendly, but none too comfortable as the horse-hair upholstery pricked our thighs and the backs of our legs, but the feather beds were bliss. There were lovely familiar smells: apples being stored in back bedrooms; tomatoes ripening on window sills; pots of geraniums and bunches of roses or chrysanthemums.

Lying in bed here was a joy, snuggled in feathers, with fresh air coming in through wide open windows, no sound but the owls and an occasional cow, and the unbroken silence of peace.

I am glad we were so familiar with these two loving, but very different, homes in addition to our own. If people have only one model for anything, it can be the start of negative comparisons – "This one is better than that one, but not as good as ours."

So it could have been with the homes I encountered in my early days of working with the PPA (Pre-school Playgroups Association) in the early 60s. Because this remarkable voluntary movement was sweeping the country so quickly, a one-off grant was made for someone to travel the country for three years and then to write a report to say what was happening. I was privileged to be that person, and because money was so tight I slept in members' homes wherever I went.

What I learned above all else was that every home was different in almost every possible way – save for the fact that it *was* 'home' to each and every child and adult who lived there. Each home and family had its own 'feel' created by those who lived together within it.

I slept in children's bedrooms, while they doubled up in each other's beds, or on improvised beds. I slept on camp beds in dining rooms, caravans in the garden, camping mattresses in store rooms, beds with their own sitting rooms in lovely old country houses, ice cold bedrooms, warm rooms with the airing cupboard, huge rooms, tiny rooms, luxurious rooms, and rooms where bean bags were the only furniture. No matter what, every family welcomed me, and I knew without doubt that I was in a loved and loving home, each of which housed a unique family.

What is more, although many had playrooms full of toys, time and time again I found the children doing all the things my sister and I had done – including every single one of the games we played after lights-out.

I begin to think that each generation of children has the natural ability to make the discoveries we made (if they are not distracted too soon by manufactured pleasures) – and it was lovely to discover that so many parents still react to these discoveries in exactly the same way as ours had done, with tolerance and a blind eye – until the moment came to say, 'enough!'

CHAPTER 4

From home to school

Learning to read

I have two memories of the pre-reading stage. One is of a happy period brought to a traumatic close, rather like a lovely family holiday spoilt on the last day by a fall from the breakwater. The other was a single moment of joyous recognition.

My memory of my first class room is as clear as a coloured photograph: tall windows down one side, a blackboard and cupboard at the end, and the wall joining the door and the blackboard enlivened by a frieze of pictures of objects that I recognised, with two black letters in the corner of each one. One letter was bigger than the other, and sometimes they were the same shape – S and s – and sometimes they were different – G and g.

Every morning the teacher walked along the line of pictures pointing with her stick and asked us what the picture was, then she gave us the name of the big letter, and the little letter, and told us what they 'said'. The trouble was that what they 'said' wasn't a proper word, just a smack of the lips, or a click of the tongue, or a humming, or a buzz, or a hiss. The sounds were so tricky that they became blurred into an almost-word: B is for ball, and b says *ber*, C is for cat, and c says *ker*, D is for dog, and d says *der* – I loved the rhythm and repetition and looked forward to this daily ritual. Then the format changed. The teacher pointed to a picture at random and called out the name of a child who had to tell the rest of the class what it was, such as, "Aitch is for hat, and aitch says *her*." When it was my turn, the inevitable happened: I couldn't jump the gap between the alphabet frieze and me, and I just cried with the enormity and hopelessness of it all.

My second memory is of the teacher walking round the class giving each of us a small alphabet card. They were made of thick cardboard, rather dark and greasy from much fingering, but the edges were still pale and almost woolly. On this particular day my card had a picture of a small umbrella, with the handle curved towards the left (I can see it distinctly still) and two identical letters, in different sizes, on the top right-hand corner. I looked at the card and knew in a glorious flash exactly what it 'said' to me. Loud and clear it said, "I want that little umbrella, and a basket-work holder to fix it to my doll's pram, and then Norah and I can take our dolls for a walk together. And I can be like her and when it rains or is too hot we can *both* put up our umbrellas to shield our children."

I have no recollection of what happened next; I can only say that I can still re-capture the joy of that moment when I suddenly 'saw' the connection between letters and the fact that they could speak to us.

After that came flash cards, and I can remember sitting cross-legged on the floor round the teacher's small chair and waiting in excitement and apprehension for the first flash card to be held up. It was all very simple: if I could 'see' the picture that I associated with the word, I knew it. If there was a complete gap between the two, I didn't.

Many years later I was appointed part-time to teach about a dozen 'backward children' in a local village school, and it quickly became apparent that a backward reader is not at all the same thing as a backward child.

In many of these children I caught glimpses of myself, and memories stirred. I had thought the reading scheme books were incredibly dull, and couldn't imagine anyone being interested in the characters or the things they did. But I was wrong. The children may not have been interested in the contents, but there came a moment for many of them when they suddenly discovered they could look at a word and say what it was. Their joy knew no bounds, like toddlers suddenly discovering they can walk, one foot in front of the other, stagger and blunder, but *doing it*. Sensing their excitement and the sudden power sweeping them along, I didn't have the heart to slow them down, or to ask questions to test their comprehension. I just let them gallop and stumble, and gallop again, and enjoyed the excitement with them; it was just a stage, and it spent itself, but the feeling of mastery stayed to see them through to the next stage.

The disadvantage of sounding out letters was brought home to me – there is no way that poorly (or even well) articulated sounds are going to turn '*ner.. ee.. ger.. her.. ter*' into 'night'. Sometimes it worked to say, "I'll tell you this one. It's 'night', and I bet you don't remember that tomorrow!" or "This is a very hard word. You might need one, or even two, more birthdays before you can remember it. Don't worry; I will tell you each time we come to it until you are ready." Sometimes it helped to create a picture, tracing the letters and saying, "Look, here is your head on the pillow, here are your legs stretching down into the bed, here are the two long curtains hanging up at the window – it's night." But best of all it worked to say, "Don't stop if you don't know a word. Just say 'earwig' and carry on. 'It is time to go to sleep. Good earwig,' said Mother. What do you think that word could be?" And in a flash back came the word, "Night!"

I think the overall lesson is that it is a case of try, try and try again in as many different ways as we can until we find something that does work. It may be that dyslexics have an advantage in this multiple approach to difficulties. We know so well what it feels like to be on the other end of the line, and we can remember what helped us.

Learning to love books, but not to read them

I loved books long before I went to school, and fortunately for us our mother loved reading aloud. We took it in turns to sit on her lap, or on the arm of the chair, and sometimes we both squashed on her lap together, each holding one side of the book and turning the pages as promptly as any pianist's sheet turner, for we knew all the stories by heart. I can feel again in retrospect scorching my leg if it came in contact with the shiny leatherette chair cover nearest to the fire. And, shame on us, trying to prise Mother's eyes open if she fell asleep.

The stock of books was not large, and they were all the more prized for that, for familiarity and repetition are the very stuff of childhood.

I had three favourites, particularly one that had belonged to Mother when she was a child, called "Stories to tell the littlest ones". The cover was dark green, the pages thick and woolly, and each story was illustrated by a wonderfully life-like sketch, each of which just happened to be, for me, the very personification of the whole story.

Another favourite was the Annual Bumper Book for Girls, given to me regularly by an Aunt. The parcel under the Christmas tree was large and heavy, which was gratifying in itself, and it, too, had the familiar thick and woolly pages. I can see now that it had nothing to recommend it from a literary point of view, but I *loved* it. Isn't that enough just sometimes? It was full of things to do, and we were actually *meant* to fill in spaces, and complete patterns, using pencils or crayons on the paper. Joining up dots to make a picture was particularly satisfying. Above all there was one particular story, told in a series of pictures contained in black line frames, each with a few lines of story underneath, extending over several pages. I asked for it again and again. I have no recollection of the story because there was only one picture I wanted to see, but we had to arrive at it by a proper progression from the beginning until we reached it (on the left hand page near the bottom on the right). The picture was of a clearing in a wood, with a fire on which rested a frying pan held by a witch in a black pointed hat, and the pan was absolutely full of fat sizzling sausages. There was a pile of wood for the fire behind the witch, and her broomstick was propped up against it, but I never focused on that. The excitement and satisfaction of reaching this particular picture never lessened. We still had to finish the story decently, but I had no interest beyond this point, and I haven't the slightest idea why it held me as it did. Children have their own reasons for their reaction to stories, and it seems reasonable enough that the reader should comply gracefully with such requests until the story loses its fascination.

A third favourite was Rupert Bear, another regular Christmas present, and there were two distinct reasons for producing this night after night. One was, could we tip the scales towards the full reading of all the text, at the bottom of the page, or would we be fobbed off with the shorter version, the rhyming couplets under each picture? A useful discovery was that if we were told there wasn't time for any more we could sometimes wheedle an extension by pleading, "Just the quick Rupert, and then no more?" The other reason for enjoying 'Rupert', I distinctly remember, was that during the course of the long version Rupert was called upon to face various dangers and dilemmas, and I knew he would be safe because he always wore his comfort scarf. I wasn't a very brave child. I liked happy endings without too much suspense along the way.

Later, a completely different reading experience came my way. Someone gave me the complete set of Beatrix Potter books, which could be stood up on the windowsill in their special open-fronted box. They were a complete contrast with anything that had gone before. Not large and heavy, but small and easy to hold; not the familiar thick pages, but crisp and shiny paper, beautiful to touch; not black line drawings, but tiny paintings of exquisite colours and detail, not boxed in with lines, nor yet free floating on a page, but gently contained nevertheless as the colours smudged out a little way beyond the central picture. Best of all, a perfect little picture on one page, and only a few lines of reading on the other, and the two were part of the same whole. Quite often I didn't know what the individual words meant, but it didn't matter for they sounded so beguiling that the picture and the sound were self-explanatory. Who cared what 'soporific' meant? It was what lettuces were, and one look at Peter Rabbit's young relations snoozing in Mr McGregor's compost heap was all I needed to know.

There is a time for stopping to explain words, but most definitely there is a time not to jolt the listening child back to reality. I can remember Mother trying to do it once or twice, and me saying, "No, don't tell me. I don't want to know," when what I really meant was, "Don't tell me. I already know, and you are spoiling it all."

So often we insult children's sensory intelligence. Some children are way ahead of us in an intuitive knowledge that does not rely on facts to get at the heart of the matter. It would be a tragedy if anyone ever tried to simplify these stories in word, colouring or detail. True, they don't appeal to all modern children, but for those who love anything in miniature, who can look and look until every last detail of the pictures registers, and who have an appreciation of beauty, and a love of words, these books are unsurpassed. If we bring children down to what we think is *their* level, we can rob them of a unique experience by bringing them down to *our* level.

142

These are the only books I remember of the being-read-to stage, so what happened next? I remember being sure I could read because I could recite the stories. Although I don't remember it, I think it must have been a shock to discover that I couldn't read a thing when I was given unfamiliar books at school. I did learn to read up to a point, but it never meant anything to me because by then I didn't want to read at home anyway – I was much too busy doing things and making things.

I remember a brief period of enjoying stories about older children at school, because by then I could relate to what it was all about: the heroine, the sneak and the bully; the importance of our team winning; the false accusations and punishments; and it all coming right in the end.

Then nothing more until '0' level English, and a miraculous new teacher who asked a thousand questions, ruined the poem or prose involved for some of us, but taught us to think as an exercise in itself. "Do you like this poem?" "Yes." "Why?" "Because of the words." "Which words?" "Ripening." "Why that word?" On and on it went, and I have yet to meet a single old boy or girl in the intervening years who has not said, "Do you remember Jean McKay? She taught me to think." What an invaluable gift to have been given!

I was always good at listening if I could relate to what was being said, and listened avidly to the teachers, and to the questions people asked, and to the answers. I asked questions of my own and somehow or other I learned from people rather than directly from the textbooks and managed to scrape through exams, but I had learned next to nothing. On our first drive through France, with my husband and children, we rounded a blind corner and there, rising up before us was a massive lump of rock, folded, striated, multi-coloured, gleaming in the bright sunlight, and I cried out loud, "The Massif Central!" And at last, for the first time, I understood. That thunderclap of knowledge was a revelation.

After that it was shock horror all the way as people discovered that

I never read. I went to get library tickets for our son before he could walk, and the Librarian asked if I needed my ticket up-dated. I said I hadn't got one and she couldn't have been more shocked if I had suddenly ripped off all my clothes – something I felt she had already done. The old guilt and inadequacy returned to engulf me, but this time there was a streak of defiance.

Shortly afterwards, I was listening to 'Woman's Hour' and a woman was talking about her childhood. She said everyone in her family permanently had their noses in books, and she never remembered going out for the day without her Mother saying, "Have you got your book and your cardigan?" This went on for years until, as she so graphically described it, "Then one day I discovered Life, and I never wanted to read another book about other people's lives. I wanted to live my own!" Another thunderclap of revelation, for I knew that was what I had always wanted, to have life and have it more abundantly, never, ever to go off at half cock. And for me this meant living in the here and now, and when I wasn't 'doing' I wanted to think, but it was *my* thoughts I wanted to think, for there were almost too many to cope with and (although I didn't understand why) I knew I had to keep abreast of them if I wasn't to sink in inner muddle. From then on I gave myself permission not to read if I didn't want to. After all, I wasn't shocked if people didn't want to garden, or cook, or make clothes for their children. Now that I know I am dyslexic, and meet an increasing number of people who share my difficulties, a pattern has emerged about who can read what, and we share a great many characteristics:

Thick books intimidate us.

So do closely typed pages with small print. We needs dots, dashes, brackets, inverted commas – anything to break up that even sheet of print.

Jargon, or high-flown language that is not part of everyday speech, puts us off our stroke.

Long sentences rob us of our confidence before we even start.

Extra descriptions, thoughts, observations or asides cloud the main issue, and we are bogged down with nowhere to go, except back to the beginning of the sentence, paragraph or even chapter.

Too many characters and places confuse us, and we have to keep skipping back to check names.

What then, you may well ask, is there left to read?

Many of us can read if we look at the words and 'hear' the author talking to us, but it only happens if he or she is telling us something we want to hear.

Many of us can read if we can identify immediately with the central character, for then we *become* them and already know slightly in advance of reading the words what we can sense comes next. I know a wonderful dyslexic mother of three who spent every day of her school life in the remedial class, who lost confidence in reading to her three young children when they reached the stage of bringing her books that she hadn't learned by heart, and who struggled in vain to read books people gave her. As she put it, "I would read a page, and then not know what it had been about, so I had to go back to the beginning again, and again, and again. There has only been one book in my life that I was able to read straight through. It was called 'Born Free' and I identified *completely* with Elsa the lioness and her cubs."

Many dyslexics can also read publications designed for people with a particular interest, for they already partly know through their own experience that they may be about to learn something of value to them. I think our reading owes more to intuition than formal reading skills; dyslexics are often very quick at picking up on clues, and our imagination is actively co-operative when we are not on guard and tensed up.

Oddly enough long and difficult names of people or places are not a problem. We just say to ourselves, "I shall never remember that, so I shan't even try to puzzle it out. I shall recognise the overall look of it next time, and can remember back to here, and hope that it all fits in."

As a measure of my reading limitation it may help to say that on holiday my husband read a book a day, while it took me the whole fortnight to read the latest Dick Francis racing stable mystery. I had to picture the layout of every trainer's stables, every racecourse, every horsebox, every owner's home and family, every jockey's friends and rivals. One book took more than the holiday because it included a plane crossing the Channel to ferry the horses to a French racecourse. I was unable to gloss over the interior of the plane because the attempted attack depended on who was hiding where. Was the trainer sitting beside or behind the pilot? Were the hay bales between them and the horses, or behind the horses? Where and how were the horses tethered? Where were the stable lads supposed to sit or sleep? Not only that, but the layout of the small private landing strip in France had to be mapped, hangar to the left or right of the runway? Woods? River? Once it was all pictured, then the action jumped off the page with the clarity of a film, and I enjoyed it each year.

My family also picture what they read, but it is instantaneous for them; slow and laborious for me.

The compensation is that many of us can 'read' people and situations much faster and more accurately than we can read books. All our senses are brought to bear, including the sixth sense. The habit of mapping and picture building enables us to see and sense the overall picture, and the individual positions of the people within the picture. From here it is sometimes possible to help those involved to map out their own pathways to a meeting point. This reading of problems, situations, relationships and possibilities continues to be one of the joys of life, and sources of our growth and development, as we slowly learn the crucial importance of which questions to ask.

Early school sums

I have great faith in children's self-motivated, uninterrupted play, for in all the years I have been watching them it has seemed to me that their inner prompting leads them to find what they need to do to restore their confidence and inner peace, to satisfy their curiosity, or to lay hold of new learning.

So it was with sums and me. I *loved* adding up, and would set myself pages of sums running from the top of the page to the bottom, with a line underneath to indicate that that was the end of the sum, and when I arrived at the answer there would be a double line as a way of signing off. I never remember asking anyone to check them for me. Red ticks and gold stars were not what I was after. I just wanted to practise this new skill.

On looking back, my mother had a quite remarkable outlook on bringing up children, especially in view of the fact that she was born in 1893. She had a feeling for play that she never lost: it was what made you happy and satisfied – including Monday wash-day, with the fire to light under the copper, to heat the water brought in from the pump, which she called her 'water party day'.

She was well content to let me do self-imposed sums because she saw how happy and satisfied it made me feel. She never looked over my shoulder, or set sums for me, or tried to get me on to the next stage, for that would have turned play into work. And woe betide any teacher who set homework! When homework was first sent home she wrote one of her famous (or infamous?) notes to say that she understood and accepted that the law required children over the age of five to attend school. But there was no law to say that school should intrude into the home, and this she couldn't allow because it would interfere with our play, which was much more valuable.

Our parents had no desire for us to 'get on'; they genuinely wanted only our happiness in all its forms and flavours – Father because he loved us and trusted Mother, and Mother because her school days had been *so* unhappy and counter-productive that she felt there had to be another way.

After a prolonged period of playing with adding-up sums, I came to the conclusion that I much preferred figures to letters. They were bigger, bolder, more simple and satisfying shapes, and there were only ten of them to remember instead of twenty-six. Also there was a clarity about working with numbers, a rightness and wrongness, and they were constant and didn't start saying something else if they were combined in different ways. At least, nothing bewilderingly different – you just had to take it on trust that once your simple numbers were multiplied by ten their names did change a bit: four became forty; six became sixty; two didn't become twoty, but twenty; and three didn't become threety but thirty.

Right through school I always had the feeling that I was a hair's breadth away from being good at maths, if only I could find the key.

Subtraction was more difficult, but at least it only involved two lines of numbers. Each morning we were given a sum card to copy into our exercise books, which was a bit tricky as I had to put it right beside my page, and hold it down firmly with one finger so that the numbers could be transferred accurately. When I had finished the sum card I could stand up and walk importantly to the front of the class to replace my finished card in the sum box, take out a new one, and walk importantly back to my seat. I remember the feeling of importance so well. I wonder why anyone ever thought children didn't like formality.

Trouble came when the sums were less simple, and the process of 'borrowing' and 'paying back' had to be mastered. Anything new filled me with anxiety, but once the new pattern of working became familiar, confidence returned.

Multiplication was more difficult still until I discovered that if, instead of trying to work out 457 multiplied by 7, I said to myself, "What are seven lots of 457?" Then all I had to do was write down 457 seven times and, hey presto! I had an adding-up sum – easy!

Years later, when I was teaching in a Child Guidance Clinic, I discovered that if I helped children to learn their tables it sometimes gave them a sense of mastery, and they enjoyed the sing-song repetition. They also loved being taught the tricks of the trade: for example all the answers to the 9 times table are numbers whose individual figures add up to 9. Not only that, but if you want to know what 7 nines are, the answer begins with the number *below* 7, which is 6 – then all you have to do is say to yourself, "It begins with 6, and it has to add up to 9, so the next figure must be 3. 7 x 9 = 63 – got it!" Their excitement and glee at learning this trick never varied. It was as though they felt they had discovered a secret way to beat the system.

It is easy to say, "But your ways take so much longer, and they are so much more complicated. Why didn't you persevere until you could do it the normal way?" But what if you *can't* do it the normal way? You either give in or you risk making a mistake that reinforces the feeling that you are no good, so you play safe and do it your way, and then you can feel pleased with yourself for having managed it.

Sometimes we need complication, to make it simple for *us*. For example, if we have to multiply 137 x 12 and we are not sure of our 12 times table, we can multiply it first by 6 and then by 2 – or decide that it would be easier still if we multiplied first by 4, and then by 3.

I continued to enjoy sums against all the odds, so long as no-one hurried me or spoke in a cross voice. I enjoyed them so much that I continued to make up and do dozens of them at home, as play.

Little did I know that I was reaching the end of my ability to find my own way of making these basic stages of maths manageable. There came a day, when I was about nine, when a greatly loved teacher wrote a new kind of sum on the blackboard. She was slow and clear as she talked us through each stage, spread over several lines of numbers. She left the sum on the board and stood quietly, as she always did, while we took it in; then she rubbed out all the lines of working and just left the original sum, and worked it out a second time; then she rubbed the workings out again, saying, "What do we do next?" at each stage. The clever ones knew immediately. I was still mesmerised. She asked, "Is there anyone who still isn't quite clear?" and up went my hand as usual. She was patience personified, and went through it again, but by then the class was beginning to heave sighs of, "She's holding us up *again*!" So when I was asked, "Is it all right now?" I fell back on the usual social lie and said, "Yes, thank you," while I sat there with the familiar feeling of dread and anticipation of what would happen next.

Miss Barnes rubbed the board clean, wrote the sum again and told us to copy it into our exercise books, then rubbed the board clean again. Sheer panic on my part. I couldn't. I kept looking at the empty board, trying to visualise the sum that had been there so recently, and then gave up in despair. I did the only thing possible, and copied the sum and answer from the girl who sat next to me. This went on for several days until she got one wrong, and so did I, in exactly the same way – and then, understandably, the saintly Miss Barnes was angry in the most public and humiliating way and ended by saying, "How *could* you cheat like that?" It was the worst moment of my life, and I couldn't get home fast enough, to burst into the house in floods of tears saying, "I cheated, and I didn't want to." Mother put her arms round me and said, "I know, I used to do it too, and felt just as you do now. Come and tell me about it."

Oh, the relief! I have no recollection of what happened next, but the sheer awfulness of the experience was alleviated by knowing that I wasn't alone in having done such a terrible thing. Someone I loved, trusted and respected had also done it, but above all she understood *why* I had done it.

I don't know whether I remembered this crucial moment sub-consciously, or whether it was my repeated experience of being grateful to the people who could recognise and identify with me in failure, inadequacy and wrong-doing, but because of it I have tried to work with children and their parents from the common ground of our vulnerability rather than my supposed strength as a trained teacher or experienced mother.

All my life I have seen delightful children lose confidence as they struggle to become what they felt they were expected to become, while their real potential dwindled. Working with parents, I saw the same thing happening with the same result – with both generations, we have to learn to join them on the level of our own vulnerability, sharing laughter as we revel in each other's mistakes. Where there is laughter there is the potential for healing and learning.

Numbers and spaces

I loved Ludo. I can still re-capture the feeling of anticipation as I opened the box, removed the stout green board, and opened it up to reveal the bold pattern covering the surface. I loved the small, smooth, translucent, red, blue, yellow and green counters, but above all I loved the big wooden dice with its rounded corners, and different patterns of black spots on all six sides.

The first stage of play was confined to shaking the dice out of its container, and saying what it 'said'. Even then I needed to touch the indentations as I counted them aloud, and only very slowly did I come to recognise the distinct pattern of dots representing the six numbers. It didn't matter. There was no hurry, and repetition is one of childhood joys at any stage. Then came the choosing of our preferred colour, and matching the counters to the background square that was 'Home'. I remember the four small white circles that exactly held the four counters, and placing them with absolute accuracy so that the white was completely covered. The precision pleased me, as though I were saying, " I can do this – good!" I remember, too, the anxiety-free interest of waiting for the shaker to tip out a six, which meant that I could leave home and stand on the doorstep. As far back as I can remember, there was always the need to reinforce words with pictures, and put the message in story form. From then on it was a matter of throwing the dice, saying what it said, and then doing what it said.

The need for time and patience is crucial. It is so easy for the adult to call out, "Five!" It isn't the number or landing place of the counter that matters. From the child's point of view each completed move is a triumph of understanding and execution, and on its completion a second or two of silent contemplation is often called for to appreciate the fact that it has been done properly. We grossly under-rate the time it takes for some children to master each small stage from picking up the shaker to setting the counter on its destined square on the board.

We glance at the distinctive pattern of dots that says 'five' and know it immediately, but some children will need to count the spots repeatedly before the moment comes when they can see and say simultaneously, "Five!"

When it is our turn to throw the dice, we need to do it with the same slow and thoughtful deliberation. If we dash off our turn in a few seconds it isn't long before the child begins to feel slow, clumsy and inadequate.

In the early stages it is enough to throw, count and move our way around the board until we reach Home again. The more often we do it, the quicker, smoother and easier it becomes, until the moment arrives to start playing according to the rules of the game. There is a whole new range of skills to be learned at that stage: learning to wait for the starting six without losing heart; learning to send and be sent home without excessive boasting or aggression; and yet learning to face up to, and come through, all those emotions, for that is part of learning to live. (It helps if the adult keeps his or her own emotions even, remembering it is by our example that children learn most of all.)

Later still comes the challenge of considering tactics: do I try to get all counters safely home as closely together as possible? Do I concentrate on one and get that home first? Do I try to keep behind my enemy, waiting to throw exactly the right number to land on him and send him home? Do I risk getting ahead of him and hope that I shan't be pounced in this same way? Do I wait just behind the enemy's doorstep, hoping to pounce on him when he throws a 6 and comes out? Or do I wait for a big throw and scuttle past his door as quickly as I can? Choices and decisions every inch of the way!

By this time an understanding of space is being exercised: a low throw means we can't travel far; a high throw helps us to cover the ground more quickly. And if we have graduated to playing with two dice, and throw a double six, we can whiz along and catch up an enemy who seemed beyond reach.

I use my Ludo skills to this day. If I am adding up a column of figures my eye darts up the column flicking from dice pattern to dice pattern, while my fingers press on my thigh as though on a computer. I know it sounds unbelievable, but I can only say it is quicker to do than explain. If I hesitate for a second I am lost, and have to start again. At the end I check with my calculator, and if it agrees, that's fine; if it doesn't I do my addition again, this time from top to bottom, and if any two of the three totals agree, that is the one I use. If not, I use the calculator again, this time with a ruler held under each line of figures on the paper as I feed them in, because I know how easy it is for me to reverse numbers.

I didn't know I was dyslexic until late in life, so I thought this process was what everyone went through, and that I was just much slower than others because I was less intelligent. Giving in wasn't an option; I just persevered until the job was done. But where would I have been without those happy hours playing Ludo? It is a game worth playing with all children, for if they can master and enjoy it you will know that they have begun to grasp the fundamentals of mathematics, which involve the understanding of numbers and space, and solving problems.

I have a friend who was nine years old when her mother became pregnant again. She recalls feeling very anxious about it on the grounds that once the baby arrived, their family would no longer be just the right number for Ludo.

Discovering I couldn't spell

I still can't spell.

I never was any good at spelling but it didn't trouble me at all because I didn't register the fact until I was seven or eight years old. On that never-to-be-forgotten afternoon I had come home from school with my end of term report. Mother opened the door looking pretty in her afternoon dress as always, and listened to the daily out-pouring of news as satchels were hung up and hands washed for the tea that was ready on the table. I handed over my report confidently and we started the meal. Towards the end Mother opened it and began to read aloud the bits she always said were the most important. "*Behaviour*: excellent; *Helpfulness*: excellent; *Attitude to work*: Brenda always tries hard." So far, fortified with bread and butter and jam, all was well. Then came the subjects, read slowly and appreciatively with no hint that some comments were more welcome than others. They were just the usual: Good, Fair, Tries hard, Imaginative story teller, has done some good Art work, all of which were equally acceptable to parents who said, and meant, that all they wanted was for us to be happy and do our best.

Then the report was handed over to me to read for myself. All went well until I reached the final summing up by the class teacher, which was to the effect that if I didn't learn to spell I would never get on in the world. I was shocked beyond belief, but a calm reassuring voice from behind the teapot said, "Take no notice. She's a silly piecan and you wouldn't want to be like her, would you?"

Like a pop-up picture Miss Saunders appeared before me: short, dumpy, pale sandy hair scraped back from a fawn face, which never showed an expression of any kind. She wore brown button-up shoes, thick fawn stockings, a fawn skirt and a fawn jumper with stripes of hard orange and dark brown going round her arms and body. No, I absolutely didn't want to be like Miss Saunders! So that was all right then.

In retrospect, this was such an uncharacteristic response from Mother that it needs an explanation. A more typical reaction would have been, "But Miss Saunders has a point. You are so good at other things, but the spelling and reading seem to cause special difficulties. Shall we try to find someone who can help you?" I feel sure that her reaction sprang from her determination to protect my self-confidence, which was still so fragile – the mere suggestion that my spelling and reading left something to be desired would have been a cause of great concern to me. I knew perfectly well that the teachers who scattered scarlet 'S's down every margin were right – but I still needed to believe that Mother was even more right in her unswerving faith in me.

On looking back, I wonder why I was so unprepared for the news. As far back as I can remember, we were given short lists of spellings to learn each night, which grew longer and more difficult as we went up the school. I quite enjoyed the ritual after tea of handing the list over to Mother who read the words slowly and clearly before handing it back to me. I repeated her reading exactly in tone and rhythm, before handing it over to her again. This time each word was read out, followed by the spelling, and I copied the process again. The next stage was more difficult as I read the word, and then tried to write it without looking back and copying from the list. I tried all sorts of ruses: making a tune to sing the letters to; trying to see if there was a picture anywhere in my mind: but in the end it was sheer repetition. Friday was testing day, and after one last practice I was ready to dash into class, still reciting to myself until the teacher asked us either to write the chosen words on paper or to stand up and recite them.

I did well in these tests, but whenever I wanted to actually use one of the words, they were never there at my pencil tip. Only one word from all those hundreds of words has stayed with me. I can still hear my mother say, " No, listen – the word is sep-<u>ar</u>-ate, not sep-<u>er</u>-ate." (If she were still alive, and it were possible, I could hear her say to groups of television presenters, "No, listen – the word is Tuesday, not Chuesday, and tube, not chube: there will be a tube strike on Tuesday.")

One other word I mastered for myself. I could remember all the days of the week except Friday, and then one joyful day as I struggled with assorted letters I had a vivid flash of a large white loaf on a breadboard with one or two slices missing, but the knife ready to cut the next slice. I can offer no explanation, or make any kind of connection; I only know that it worked. I could recognise and write 'Friday' from then on.

If I can see a picture, I can remember. I can't 'decide' on a picture; it has to flash into being by itself. I decided to keep quiet about my Friday breadboard in case I was laughed at, but it seemed to me that if it helped, and wasn't doing anyone any harm, I could just add it to my private list. So I did. It is there still.

CHAPTER 5

The cycles of deprivation and privilege

If you have read this far, I hope there have been episodes that led some of you to say, "I remember doing that!" as you drifted away on the invaluable tide of your own memories. But it is inevitable that some of you will have thought, "Just how privileged is *that*? It is completely irrelevant to me and my life-style today – just *who* does she think she's writing for?"

Don't think I haven't felt anxious on this score, but I had a job to do – to discover if early family life can make a difference to those of us who later discover we have learning difficulties. I had to recall, think and write about my own childhood because it is the only one I know. My thinking took me back to the early playgroup days, in particular the early seventies, when that wonderfully apt phrase, "the cycle of deprivation" hit us all with the ring of truth.

But pendulums swing equally both ways, and my problem has been: if there is a cycle of deprivation, doesn't there also have to be a cycle of privilege? If so, what is the nature of the *privileges* we would wish to promote?

As far as I can see, these two loaded words – *deprived* and *privileged* – have changed their meaning, slightly but significantly, over the years. What often hasn't changed is some people's emotional reaction to both, but that too is becoming more informed.

I was born in 1920 and for me the face of deprivation was fixed when we used to go by coach through the East End of London. Some of the children went bare-foot even in the winter, their dirty little feet blue with cold. The luckier ones had boots – sometimes sizes too big, tied on with strips of rag in a figure of eight under the boot and around their legs. Sometimes they were much too small and the stitching had been cut to allow cramped toes to protrude. Clothes too were handed down. Arms and legs stuck out of jackets and trousers, or the garments hid hands in sleeves that hung down nearly to the pavement.

The women mostly wore drab, black skirts, aprons and shawls. Often the legs that showed beneath were 'bowed' with rickets through a lifetime of malnutrition. It was frightening to see. Only then did I understand what people meant when they said, "*You could drive a pig between her knees.*"

I was also shocked at one stall we passed regularly. Swinging from their long scraggy necks from the stall's cross-rail were plucked chickens that were nothing but skin and bone. I asked Mother why anyone bought them instead of choosing nice fat ones like Grandma's. And when she said, "Because they don't have enough money to buy anything bigger," then being *'poor'* became real.

We didn't pay any money for our chickens; they were just 'there' in the chicken run. Mother didn't hide anything, but she offered a crumb of comfort by saying, "One of those scraggy birds would make a large saucepan of beautiful chicken soup, with bread and vegetables, enough to feed the whole family." This rang true, for I always watched the equally skinny but lively children as they dashed along the gutter and round the stalls to pick up cabbage leaves, the odd squashed orange or dropped potato, or anything they could cadge from the stall holder. And very pleased with themselves they looked as they dropped them into their bags and scuttled home with their contribution to dinner.

My memory of this stretch of road, in all weathers, is so sharply etched in my mind, it comes back to me still, whenever I am confronted by comparisons.

The last time it flashed into my mind was not so long ago, when I watched a brief clip from a TV interview with a very young mother. She was in a council flat that had been allocated to her, complete with furniture and carpet. Her baby was lying on a brightly cartoon-covered mattress on the floor, an arch hung with swinging mobiles over his head. As his nappy was being changed, the teenager said in an aggrieved voice, "If I don't get more money, I shan't be able to buy him the educational toys and books he needs. He's going to start his life deprived." It occurred to me the child might well grow up to be deprived – not because she can't buy what she *thinks* he needs, but because she doesn't yet *understand* what he needs.

As I see it, true privilege has little or nothing to do with financial, social or intellectual status, still less with possessions. It is to do with core family values and relationships. Mercifully, the 'cycle of privilege' embodied in good strong family life and values is as deeply entrenched (even if in dwindling numbers), in *every* type of community, right across the country, as the more talked-about 'cycle of deprivation'.

Before these family values disappear through lack of recognition and appreciation, we should try to rid ourselves of out-dated habits of thought and ask ourselves where the real privileges lie.

If the bond between children and dominant safety-figures in their lives (be they mother, father, grandparents or exceptional 'others') is one that inspires security, love and trust, then I am not sure that anything else is of importance to the children compared with this greatest of privileges.

Recently, someone in authority felt that the loved and happy children of parents who were loving but of low intelligence should be removed to give them 'a better chance'. *A better chance of what?* Fortunately, there was such an outcry from a wide variety of parents that the idea wasn't carried out. Those who protested certainly had their priorities right.

Other examples of 'deprivation' come to mind.

I remember a bus queue at the end of the war and a young mother in front of me said to her friend, "Just as soon as we are rid of our ration books, I'm going to see to it that our kids don't grow up as deprived of everything as we have been. They can eat sweets until they come out of their ears. I'll give them all the presents they want without having to wait for birthdays and Christmas."

I hoped it was just a (fairly) natural reaction and that common sense would re-assert itself. Rationing was a necessary, temporary deprivation and if the parents of those young mothers hadn't helped their children to understand the connection between food convoys, rationing and lives, then I think they were *deprived* of a proper preparation for life and living. Are they going to resent every curb on their superficial desires later on and expect compensation in kind?

And what about the 'privileged' homes where there is a TV in every bedroom? Some parents have said to me, "They have to be in their bedrooms by eight and it's lights out at nine. Often when we go up to say goodnight and tuck them in, the lights are already off and they are asleep." Other parents have said, "As long as they are in their rooms by eight, so we can have a bit of peace and quiet, we don't bother about lights out – they'll go to sleep when they are ready." But what if they aren't ready until the early hours of the morning, stumble off to school without breakfast and fall asleep at their desks?

Although a TV in the bedroom indicates financial privilege, what counts is why it is there and how it is managed. If the reasons are not thought through, and the necessary effort isn't put into managing the children's experience, the 'privilege' can become a source of deprivation.

The first family had decided that by eight o'clock the day had been long enough for the children, but recognised also that they might not be ready for sleep. The compromise was for them to get ready for bed and then watch TV for up to an hour as they quietened down. The in-built discipline was that, having agreed to this plan, the children had to respect the deadline and be ready for the off-switch. (There is no point in agreements if they are not kept.) But the manner in which the deal was monitored was a loving visit to, "say goodnight and tuck them in".

The second family just felt that by eight o'clock they wanted "a bit of peace and quiet" (fair enough!), but they didn't take any responsibility for implementing a deadline in view of school the next day. The children were left to make decisions for which they hadn't been prepared.

I see 'privilege' not as the simple opposite of 'deprivation', but as opposite ends of a line along which, at some point, the balance can sometimes shift.

Sometimes the line is very long. In my lifetime I have witnessed the effects on parents and children of multiple deprivation: poor housing, lack of food, overcrowding and poor hygiene, all leading to low resistance to infection and early death. And now I see the result of over-indulgence in the wrong kind of food, lack of exercise, and lowered resistance to infection caused possibly by over-cleanliness, as sprays against this and that invade our homes. It is shocking to someone of my generation to hear that today's parents may outlive their obese children.

What we often miss is that even in the dirtiest and most apparently deprived homes there are some wonderful families – and in what might seem the most enviable surroundings there can be the most damaging relationships.

There is nothing wrong in parents wanting to do their best for their children. But we must think carefully about this word 'best' before things backfire. Too much that is valuable may be by-passed; too many roots may be cut; too many aspirations may be built on shaky foundations.

The young woman who brought this into focus for me was sitting in an unusually turbulent playgroup conference, in a northern town renowned for its 'deprivation'. The burning issue of the day was, 'Should playgroups teach reading before school?'

The majority were against it, knowing children and parents together need to fill in the gaps in their experience before 'going on'. I had been trying to explain all this, when up jumped an exceedingly angry young woman shouting, "You don't understand! My dad was a milk roundsman and my mum was an officer cleaner. My husband and I passed the Eleven Plus, so we're now middle class and we are *not* going to allow our children to fall back down the ladder. They have got to be taught to read to give them a head-start when they go to school."

It was an eye-opening moment and I understood so much more than she was saying. I have wished many times that I could go back to that moment. I would have tackled it differently.

I would have thanked her for her courage in speaking for so many others and then said something like, "Before we pick up on your concerns, let's just go back a bit. Your two sets of parents clearly did a very good job in bringing you up so well. You were hard-working, naturally bright and good communicators. You are now loving and ambitious for your own children and deeply involved in your own playgroup, taking responsibility for helping your own and other people's children to develop. Can you help us to see the contribution your own parents made to your life? What will you always be grateful for?"

Then I would have opened it up to everyone else. What, in retrospect, did all their parents give and teach them that they valued and wanted to pass on?

Only then would we go on to the negatives: "What didn't you like? Have you avoided it with your children? Do you suddenly realise you are doing exactly the same thing? If so, is it because it suddenly makes sense or because you have done it without realising it?"

I know I haven't yet finished thinking about and clarifying my understanding of privilege, but I can't get any further at the moment.

What I do know with certainty is that family patterns are deeply ingrained and 'cycles of privilege' such as these are fortunately just as influential as 'cycles of deprivation'. Genetically and historically, our past is contained within us, and is already part of our children. The Bible has it that "the sins of the fathers are visited upon the children, even unto the third and fourth generation," but it is equally true to say that the positive aspects of inheritance are just as strong and need to be recognised.

We can't usually control our children's genetic inheritance, but we are definitely responsible for the way we bring them up. The manner of children's upbringing, their standards, values, diligence in the face of adversity, their ability to delay gratification a little, and to be protected from 'boredom' by the contents of their own heads – all of these qualities have their first chance of being established, as seeds to be nurtured to seedlings, before school.

If families do these things for their children, then *both* generations are privileged – and teachers have a strong foundation on which to build.

I am painfully aware that an increasing number of today's children have little or no continuity in their lives – some have lived through two marriages on each side of their family. Sometimes the birth parents have made huge efforts to be there in their children's lives – but sometimes there is bitterness and children are 'used' by their parents in order to get at one another.

If you are one of these children, don't despair. Life offers us many chances to repair the damage, and it usually comes through people we meet as we live on. Keep an eye open for them. It might be a teacher, or a neighbour, or some unexpected 'other' who rings a bell of recognition for us – a sudden feeling that, "This is someone who understands; I can talk and they will listen."

My life has been full of such people. (No parents can be the perfect answer for the whole of our lives.) I look upon them as 'sent, meant and lent' for the duration of the next stage of my life. When a new relationship like this is as 'right' as it is unexpected, everything fits like a crossword – 'up and down' clues fit neatly into 'across' clues, leading to a discovery of mutual benefits. We each need a series of these special people, but we have to learn to look out for them, benefit from all they can teach us, and let them go in the fullness of time. There will be others!

CHAPTER 6

The responsibilities of adults

Digging our cabbage patch

My sister Pauline and I were very close all our lives. How could it not be, when we had shared so much, so happily, together? We took very seriously our responsibilities for bringing up our own children, especially in view of the peer pressures that were mounting all the time.

We spent a lot of time over the years 'digging our cabbage patch', by which we meant going over familiar ground because it was nostalgic and fun, but also because we sometimes had cause to ask ourselves questions that we hadn't addressed before. We had discovered that the answers were often rooted in our childhood, and we were the only two people who were intimately aware of the sub-soil of our family life. This was our very personal cabbage patch, to be dug and double-dug and re-seeded, and harvested at intervals, throughout our lives. Our sessions together always led to new insights, and more thinking to be done. One day when we parted Pauline said, "I wonder if there is any more to discover in our cabbage patch," and I said, "Surely there can't be – do you think we have finally got there?" We hadn't, of course!

During the course of one of these days, we were discussing the upbringing of our own children – which values had stood the test of time, and which needed to be adapted in changing times? We had both been able to replicate for our children the simplicity of our early years before school, and found we were reluctant to lower certain standards or to compromise certain values. This meant we had to ask ourselves questions about the 'freedom' we both felt we had had in which to explore and expand. Had we really been as free as we imagined? Or was it freedom within limits? If so, is this where up-bringing comes into its own?

Based on our shared thinking, we identified the essential elements that we had tried to pass on to our children. We recognised that there were many areas we hadn't touched on – we both felt our lack of culture and our ignorance on a huge range of subjects. But we also felt that we had been 'well brought up' and that the essential elements were still in place to pass on. We also felt that we 'knew our place' – as descendants of peasant stock, deeply rooted in the soil of East Anglia – and the rightness of this pleased us both very much. What follows are the basic elements we identified.

Love and security

My sister and I agreed that what children need above all else are love and security. This means unconditional love and over-all security. It isn't enough to *be* loved and to know that we are safe; children need to *feel* loved and secure and sometimes there is a gap between the two.

We both recalled an incident we had never shared before. Our memories of it were identical. The *circumstances* of our discovery were very privileged indeed – but its *relevance* to our lives, and to those of all children who discover this same truth, is much more widely shared.

Father wanted to talk farming with his brother who farmed about ten miles away and we all went with him. In the cool of the evening, Mother said she was going to walk over the back meadow to the wood and did anyone want to go with her? We both did, so we set off accompanied by somebody's pet goat.

We had reached the middle of the field, when ten great cart horses were led on halters from the stables, groomed, fed, watered and about to be let loose at the end of their day's labours. They did what they always did: tossed their heads, kicked up their heels and galloped to freedom. On this occasion they saw the goat and headed in our direction.

We both recalled being terrified but Mother whacked the goat on the rump and sent him dashing off for the wood and then said calmly, "We'll all stand quietly just where we are." Pauline and I remembered shutting our eyes, standing as close to Mother as we could get, and each holding one of her hands.

Forty iron-clad hooves thundered up behind us, and we could both recapture how the ground shook beneath our feet, and then they had swept in a curve around us to follow the running goat.

We opened our eyes to see the goat disappear safely into the wood and the horses brought to a standstill. Would they turn and chase us instead? Mother said, "Now we'll just walk quietly back to the gate." So we did.

There had been countless memories of knowing that we were loved, but this was the moment when we *knew* that as long as Mother (or Father) were with us, then we were safe.

Oddly enough, even if we hadn't been physically safe and the horses had knocked us over and trampled on us, we knew there was a sense in which we would still have *felt* safe – as long as we were both still tightly held, and all close together.

TV correspondents and camera men bring us daily face to face with personal suffering caused by war and by natural disasters such as floods, earthquakes, volcanoes, drought, fire and storms – followed by injury, starvation, disease and death. They show us groups of fleeing or stranded victims who often have nothing left in the world but each other. They may be starving, sick, wounded, infirm, heart-broken and without hope – but look at the faces of the children enclosed within their parents' arms and you see nothing but trust.

It is a familiar truth that 'perfect love casts out fear'. People who experience this quality of love, whatever their circumstances, are privileged.

Unhurried watching time

After unconditional love and security, what we valued most was being given all the time we needed to just watch.

Watch what....? Two birds fighting for possession of a worm; men digging a hole in the road – so deep you could see the pipes buried at the bottom; chips spitting and bubbling when they were dropped into the fat at the fish and chip shop (just look at a toddler's rapt face as he watches this from the height and safety of a parent's arms); or a gardener digging up his potatoes; or a car being filled up with petrol; a dog cocking his leg against a lamp-post; a leaf falling from a tree – not like an apple when it is dropped, but slowly, twirling and floating its way down.

We need to remember that everything in the world, however commonplace it might seem to us, is at some time uniquely new to every child seeing it for the first time – and the second, third and subsequent times, too, when they come across it under different circumstances or in a different guise. Dogs, for example, can be huge (to them), gentle Labradors, or small, yappy terriers, or shaggy monsters, or shiny sausages on very short legs, or strange-looking poodles. All go by the name 'dog' – but how can you be expected to recognise the different types without repeatedly meeting them? What makes them different? And what experiences build up in your mind to make you like them or fear them?

I knew a mother who used to sling a collapsible stool between the handlebars of her big pram and when out for the daily walk, if her small son wanted to stop and look at something, she let him. If it was clear that a few seconds wasn't going to be enough, then she would prop the baby up, seat herself comfortably on her stool, get her crochet out of her bag and enjoy the peaceful interlude with the children.

The world has speeded up so much since we were children that there isn't unlimited *watching time* available these days. Shops shut, buses have to be caught, trains met, and sometimes our children are required to co-operate, reluctant as they may be. But in return, if we understand their genuine need to watch and if we deliberately aim to build valuable watching time into their day, we can do it.

People are either amazed or disbelieving that I am able to recall incidents that happened from before my first birthday. We both could. I wonder now whether it had anything to do with the fact that as children we were so unhurried. We had time to savour so much that children of today are rushed through – and it was this that was my salvation, I am sure.

The value of silence

When we watched, we didn't want to be interrupted – least of all by a stream of 'teaching' talk along the lines of, "I wonder what he's going to do next," and, "Look how he's ....." or, "Would you like to do that one day?" For goodness' sake! How can we answer questions, when we haven't yet taken in what is happening?

This is precisely *why* we are watching. Before questions arise, the chances are that our eyes and ears are already taking in the over-all picture and we are now being beguiled by the rhythm of what is being done. We are simply not ready to be questioned yet.

We also enjoyed silence when we were alone. No background music. No constant stream of chat, let alone a running commentary from parents on anything and everything: "What are you doing?" ... "Don't touch that." ... "I shouldn't get out any more things – you'll only have to put them away." ... "Would you like me to help you?" ... "See if you can do this." ... "Slowly! Here, let me show you."

When this kind of example is offered to parents, they are rueful – but they also add to the selection, particularly in the area of "Careful!...Hurry up...Quickly now." I remember one mother saying, "The awful thing is that we are so *nice* about it ! We are told we have to talk to our children and we mean to be friendly, not boring! But it can become a habit..."

Silence was, and still is, particularly important to me. I need time to take in, ponder and make connections, and to repeat the process again and again before I can feel I have learned something – or, at the very least, that I am *on* to something. As I can't go back to books to check, I have to go back inside my head.

Our personal silence wasn't just absence of noise; sometimes noise is part of what we are watching, like the powerful noise of a pneumatic drill as it breaks up a road surface, or the thundering of waves, followed by the noise of stones being drawn back off the beach and into the path of the next wave.

Sometimes, silence can seem threatening. I can remember waking in the dead of night, straining my ears to hear the sound of a snore or the creak of a bed-spring and – when I couldn't – a flash of panic. Had I been abandoned in an empty house?

Sometimes, silence can be magical. In the hot hush of a Mediterranean afternoon, I remember wandering into an ancient olive grove in Greece. On a sudden impulse, both my husband and I stood still and listened to silence. Not a bird to be heard; not a breath of breeze to stir the leaves above us; not a crackle of dry leaves underfoot, or an aeroplane, or people calling in the distance – just the warm scent of silence.

My husband said later it was the first time in his life that he had ever *heard* silence – and I knew exactly what he meant. This wasn't an absence of sound. Rather, it was a living, breathing silence, and I had felt I was part of the 'one-ness' of everything that was, or ever had been or was to come.

An Eastern mystic described such moments as "'the expansion of oneself into the living ether," and some of you will have experienced them for yourselves in more familiar surroundings, for they are not confined to beautiful places, or even happy times.

One of the most valuable times of silence for me occurs when I wake in the night and lie in a state between waking and sleeping. My mind floats free; not consciously focussing on anything but with shadowy images swirling slowly across my inner eye; and then one or two come into focus and I hear faint snatches of conversation from me to I know not who. Sometimes, I drift back into sleep; sometimes, I wake fully and everything is lost. But just sometimes, I can hold that moment long enough to discover that I have found the key to some problem that has troubled me for a long time.

This is only the first stage in thinking through, but once I have got this far, what I have grasped won't go away. I can put it aside, bring it back, alter or amend it here and there, put it away again in the hay-box of my mind, and know that with each up-dating, I am growing in understanding.

Extenuating circumstances

We were even more fortunate than we knew at the time to have had people's behaviour and way of living explained to us, especially as the explanations always gave everyone the benefit of the doubt.

One particular episode comes to mind.

I had been formally invited to tea by Rosalie's mother, whom I had never met, who lived four doors away from us in a house I had never visited. The minute I was inside, and the door was closed, I felt anxious and wanted to go home.

I had never heard the words 'austere', 'stern', 'repressed' or 'wary' before, but I *experienced* all of them before tea was over.

Mrs O'Connor led me into the kitchen where tea was prepared and I was seated next to Rosalie, but she wasn't the happy smiling friend I had at school.

Five of her brothers and sisters filled all the other chairs except one. Their mother sat at the head of the table behind a very large teapot.

There were plates of thick bread spread with a scraping of strange-tasting butter, a small dish of jam and a plate of biscuits.

We all ate in silence and I ate very slowly because I knew I didn't want a second slice of bread with what was spread on it. Suddenly, the door opened quietly and the eldest child, a girl called Wendy, slipped in and sat down silently. She was evidently expected to be late, because her mother just got up to fetch a plate with two slices of bread and butter from the dresser and put it in front of her.

One by one, the rest of us had been offered a biscuit. When I had finished mine, Mrs O'Connor said, "Would you like anything else to eat?" and I replied, "Please may I have another biscuit?" and the answer was, "No, you have had yours and that one is Wendy's." I was mortified. How could I have been so greedy? It was all I could do not to cry, but the moment we all left the table I said, "Thank you for having me. I must go now," and fled home.

On recounting all this I found that although part of my distress was certainly being made to feel that I had behaved badly, an even greater part of it was feeling upset that Rosalie had such a horrid mother.

Mother assured me that all of the O'Connor children were greatly loved and beautifully brought up. She added that, "Poor Mrs O'Connor must get very tired looking after a family of nine. They aren't as lucky as us, having eggs and milk and vegetables from the farm, so buying food for all of them must be very expensive. No wonder there isn't enough money for treats when friends come to tea."

Years later, I learned the meaning of those wise and wonderful words, *extenuating circumstances,* but it was through explanations like these that we began to learn that we didn't always read the situation accurately and that people didn't always want or have or do things our way – but even if they did, sometimes they couldn't, for all sorts of reasons. And sometimes, *we* would love to do and have things that other people did and had but likewise we couldn't for all sorts of reasons.

Respecting children's instincts

Bringing up children to see other people and their behaviour in a positive rather than a negative light is fine. On the other hand, their genuine likes and dislikes shouldn't be over-ruled.

Children's instincts are often intuitively accurate. If we want to encourage the growth and development of this invaluable gift, we need to tread carefully.

I remember a session on a playgroup course when a mother came in saying, "I have a problem. Please can you all help me?" Her in-laws were coming for lunch the following Sunday (a rare, and often fraught, occasion). "The children don't like this granny much and they don't want to kiss her. My husband says it would mean a lot to her and why can't I make them give her a quick kiss on the cheek?"

There was a chorus of approval for this solution before a few people began to offer other points of view. "How can you *make* one person kiss another?" "Why should they hurt Gran's feelings and upset their dad?" "It is very selfish to refuse such a small gesture that would mean so much."

At this point up spoke someone who talked from her own deepest personal experience. "I'll tell you why. Because it can be revolting! When I was a child, I had to submit to being enveloped and squashed into an overflowing and flabby bosom and she smelt of old lady and she had prickly whiskers on her chin and layers of chins that wobbled. Every time, I tried not to breathe and willed my parents to save me — but they never did. I felt betrayed."

So far everyone had identified with the parents, but now others began to recall how they had felt on similar occasions.

They had been betrayed too. Then someone expressed a different doubt: If we go against a child's instincts and make it an issue of, "You must be kind to others," are we going to make it difficult for them later to have the courage and inner authority to say "No" when they should rightly say 'no' to an inappropriate kiss?

The best we could come up with before the Sunday deadline was to suggest that one of the parents could phone during the week to say that they were looking forward to the visit but thought it might be helpful to explain beforehand that both (or one) of the children were going through a 'phase' of not wanting to kiss or be kissed, and that they were sure she would understand.

Not very satisfactory possibly but at least we all went away with some quite big issues to think about.

Children's judgements are of course not infallible, any more than anyone else's, and they need adult help sometimes to find a way to reconsider. But we also must be willing to reconsider in the light of children's reactions and observations.

Pauline and I recalled making sweeping negative statements about other people along the lines of "I hate her. She's unfair...beastly....soppy; she tells tales to other people....sucks up to the teacher...." On one of these occasions we were in the dining room of our farming grandfather and he was present. He just looked up from his paper and said, "Everyone in the world is better than you at something."

We hadn't realised he was listening and were discomforted to the point of running out into the garden. But once there we began to compare notes, taking it in turns to name someone we didn't like and trying to think of a single thing they did better than us. As so often happens, it began to degenerate into farce and our suggestions became idiotic and none too polite. Nevertheless, the seed had been sown and we agreed that over the years it had taken root.

Right and wrong

We had very few rules. Reduced to their simplest, they came down to :

We mustn't hurt people;

We mustn't hurt animals;

and

We mustn't damage property or belongings.

The latter was brought home to us by our other grandfather, a carpenter turned businessman. He used to say, "A man's work must be respected." (We knew this included women, because he wouldn't allow playing with or wasting the food that Grandma had cooked.) Once, when I was about ten, I came back with, "I thought that was factory made," and he said, "It was, but a man had to stand by the machine in case it broke down. A man's time has to be respected too."

On looking back, my sister and I agreed with this basic simplicity of morality. We also agreed that the first step was to consider that to young children, "Right" is what pleases parents and is rewarded with hugs and smiles and approving words like 'good' and 'clever'. "Wrong" is what changes parents' responses quite dramatically. Their voices are raised (and can be frightening). We may be grabbed, shaken or pulled away from what we are doing and words like 'bad' and 'naughty' are used.

Mystifyingly, on some days, something said or done is met by warm laughter between the adults present and although words like 'bad' and 'naughty' may be used, they are said in a jokey sort of way: "You're a bad, bad boy!" or, "Who's a naughty rascal then?" On another day, exactly the same action or word is repeated (without an audience) and the reaction is one of anger. (This is particularly so in reaction to swear words.)

Any child who can depend on a consistent reaction to what is said and done is truly privileged.

Learning that "No" means no

We both felt that it was an essential element in learning about morality that children should understand that "No" means no. Not "Maybe," or "Coax me a little bit and I'll change it to yes,"' or, "Please don't push me too hard; you know that I give in when you've worn me down to desperation point and then I feel frightened that I am losing control."

We also felt it had been important to us that we didn't just remember 'no' as something inflicted on us from on high, almost on a whim. Sometimes, we asked for it! It wasn't just a question of obedience or disobedience, but of the part we had played in bringing the crisis to a head.

I remember clearly several different occasions when my behaviour was sparked by my inability to accept 'No', or circumstances when neither parent nor child had been to blame initially.

The earliest was a party that I missed, just through bad luck really. I *loved* parties. Especially Monica Middleton's – her mother and aunties were lovely, the party games went with a swing and the tea was magnificent. I woke up early on the party day, full of excitement, took off my nightie and found I was covered in red spots.

I went to show mother and she said, "German Measles – I'm afraid that means you won't be able to go to the party this afternoon." I cried, begged and pleaded, and said the spots wouldn't show. Mother was adamant. Even if the spots didn't show, the children at the party could still catch my measles, and they could take the measles home to other children, including babies.

I kept up my crying and pleading until quite suddenly Mother's voice changed. She stopped being adamant-but-sympathetic and snapped, "Stop making this silly fuss. You are not going to the party – and that's that." I stopped in mid-squawk and can recapture distinctly the relief I felt. Being a drama queen is hard work and I was glad it had been brought to an end. The rest of the day was perfectly ordinary – no compensation of any kind – until tea time and then came the suggestion, "Shall we have cinnamon toast by the fire?"

The fire was perfect for toasting and the twisted wire toasting forks were ready in the hearth. All's well that ends well – but "silly fusses" were off the agenda from then on, except for one or two more of the short and sharp variety.

One day, I fell heavily in the garden and the result was a dirty and quite bloody gravel rash. So indoors I dashed, a silly fuss in full swing with cries of, "Make it better!" The response was a calm voice saying, "Wait a minute and listen, because I have something to say." So I listened and heard, "Pain is your friend telling you that something is wrong, so first we have to listen to see what your friend is trying to tell you. Then when we know, I will try to make it better if I can."

She lifted me up on the draining board, removed my shoe and sock and said, "Let's start right down here and see what we can learn. Can you wriggle your toes?" I could and I did. Then it was, "Can you move your foot up and down ... and round?" I could and I did. Then it was gentle pressure on random places up my leg. All was still well. But as the gentle probing got near the knee, I began to say, "Be careful, you're hurting me!" Mother said, "Well, I don't think any harm has been done, but we can't leave the dirt there. We need to see what is underneath. I'm sure you could clean up better than me, so I'll fill the bowl with warm water and get you some cotton wool and you can see what you can do." I much preferred doing it myself, because I knew whether or not I was hurting myself. The warm water was pleasant and soon the whole of my knee was blood- and dirt-free and it looked much better. What is more, it didn't hurt.

The next bit I dreaded, but I knew that there was absolutely no way I could evade the application of iodine. The only option I had was to screw up my eyes, grab hold of something so tightly that it hurt and wait for the sting of the swift painting. At least this way I got to be told I was brave!

Pauline and I both remembered how the interest in the detective trail intrigued us and how it obliterated the panic of pain.

Another time we were all due to go to the Essex Show – our favourite day of the year, after birthdays and Christmas. We had to be there in time for the grand parade of prizewinners at half past four. We almost always had one or even two prize-winning carthorses and it was unthinkable that we wouldn't be there, sitting on our straw bales to cheer Cootie and Charley as they proudly led their beautiful Suffolk Punches around the ring adorned with silk rosettes.

The plan was that I would come home from school as quickly as I possibly could and we would all be off and away by 3.30 pm to cover the few miles to the show ground.

But, alas, I forgot. I dawdled home, chatting to friends and stroking cats, and when I finally arrived, there was only the next-door neighbour waiting to let me in. I asked where everybody was and was told, "They waited as long as they could." This caused a devastating silly fuss, all the worse because I had brought it on myself. I hadn't done as I was told and I had no one but myself to blame.

This kind of 'punishment' brought upon ourselves is infinitely more potent than being punished as a kind of 'tit for tat' exercise. It is a real step forward in learning to accept responsibility for our actions. I think of this as the discipline of consequence, or the discipline of If,

Then and Therefore: *If* I don't carry out my part of this carefully explained plan, *then* there may be a backlash that I haven't foreseen; *therefore* I will listen carefully and ask myself what might happen if I forget. In this case, missing the deadline would have such distressing consequences that I would have reminded myself at intervals throughout the day!

The next time I remember whooping up a silly fuss was when I went home from school to burst in say, "Maisie and I are going up to London for the day on Saturday." The response was a sharp, "You are doing no such thing." I was secretly thankful. All the way home I had been trying to plot our course: Liverpool Street, the Underground (Was I sure about the stations? I hated the escalators!) and then where? Hamley's Toy Shop for a look around? I hadn't given money a thought. I was just loving the excitement of the idea. I gave up on the silly fuss very quickly but reproduced a mini version next morning when I met Maisie and said, "She won't let me – she always spoils everything!" I felt mean and disloyal, and what I said was a whopping lie – but I still said it!

If we can remember how we felt in these early struggles to be honest and fair and reliable and responsible, we will surely be able to avoid saying in an accusing voice, "If you own up, I won't be cross." For goodness' sake, parental or teachers' voices proclaim that they already *are* cross, *and* disbelieving; they may well be twice our height and they can win all the arguments – do they really need to wipe the floor with us?

We agreed that we much preferred, "Never mind how it happened or who did it. Let's just put our heads together to try to work out what we can do to put matters right."

The intriguing sense of touch

Children's physical, intellectual, emotional and social development are now talked about, written about, observed, measured – and even, in some areas, tested – before names are even put down for nursery school. But not a word, often, about the joy our senses bring us.

And what about the seemingly forgotten sense of touch? The development of touch is almost a no-go area. Could this be because it isn't as simple and obvious as it seems?

Touch, feel and sensation are often inter-twined, and our empathy with children is blunted if we recognise 'touch' only as something we explore with our fingers or against our skin (like the soft piece of satin ribbon that we rubbed on our top lip as we sucked our thumbs).

We are all familiar with the fact that some children don't like their hands to feel sticky or caked in mud. Some of us might remember reaching out to touch a beautiful piece of brocade in the scrap box, only to find our fingers cringing away at the first touch of its metallic scratchiness. But we seem less aware that children may hate tapioca pudding not necessarily because they don't like the taste, but because they can't bear the feel of slime in their mouths.

Often, touch can't be divorced from feeling. Our fingers can stroke the soft, short fur of a guinea pig, but if we pick it up there is an extra dimension as we cup our hands round a warm, firm little body, and yet another dimension if we tuck it under our chin for extra comfort as we pour out all our current woes.

What do you remember about the touch and feeling of being

cuddled or tickled or having your tummy blown on? Of being smiled at, sung to? Of being stripped of clothes and lowered into a bath and immersed in warm water? Of being freed from wet soggy nappies to kick in the air and smile up at the familiar face bending over you? Is it really true that 'anyone can change a nappy'? Physically, probably, yes; emotionally, probably not.

What do you remember about motion? The arc of movement of a swing; the up and down of a see-saw; being thrown up in the air by a strong pair of arms, paddling along astride a toy on wheels; jumping over a stick on the ground. Have you ever seen the concentration on a child's face as a supreme effort is made to launch a whole body into the air with both feet off the ground at the same time?

Weight is another mystery. Why can't I lift it? Can I move it? If so, by pushing with my hands, or with the whole of my body trying to help? Or loading it bit by bit into my barrow or pram, or the trailer behind my trike? It takes time and constant repetition to learn how to tackle the problem of shifting something, and to recognise the 'feel' of resistance or yielding, and to respond appropriately.

Underneath our skin we have muscles and joints, and the more we use them, in the everyday context of living, the stronger and more co-ordinated they become – and we don't even know we have them.

I could look up my dictionary – which I have just done – and tell you that 'kinetic energy' is 'the energy which a body possesses by virtue of being in motion'. But what is the point? We may learn to use certain technical terms, and if we can use them in context we may kid ourselves that we understand what we are talking about. But this might not be so, unless we can relate it directly to children's experience. Knowing the correct words is much less important here than being sufficiently tuned in to children to identify with their struggles and to appreciate the tenacity with which they try, try and try again to achieve their self appointed goal. We will then remind ourselves not to interfere with their efforts (unless they give up in despair and ask for help), and not to assume they 'ought' to know how to do something because they are four, or because Cousin Bill can do it, or because it is 'easy' (for us).

Even if the problem of shifting something isn't one of strength, it can be due to other causes. There is the strange experience of lifting something through air and then trying to lift it from liquid up into air – especially if the liquid has got inside it. I remember a beautiful celluloid swan we had at bath time. We could see it, touch the ridged surface with our fingers, and lift it up by the slender neck or by holding it between two hands (not because it was heavy but because the wings made the body too wide for the fingers of one hand to encompass it). Then it met with an accident and a hole gaped in the wing area – if water splashed into it, the swan began to settle lower into the water and, at a given moment, it suddenly sank to the bottom of the bath. At that point it needed two hands to lift it out of the water – this time because the water inside made it heavy.

Speaking for ourselves, my sister and I agreed we were glad we had only one toy in our bath (in addition to our face flannels, a sponge, a nail brush and a wooden bath rack). If we had had more, our concentration would have been spread between them all, and we wouldn't have been able to make the detailed observations that we both remembered so well in relation to our swan.

I think I speak for a great many dyslexics and for others who also rely heavily on their sensory memories of touch and 'feel' to extend their learning, and then pass it on to others in graphic word pictures. A few weeks ago, an engineer came to find and rectify a long-standing fault in the fridge/freezer. I gave him the symptoms, answered his questions, and then sat and watched him go to work. (I do still watch!)

He gave me a running commentary: "I've met this problem with this model several times now. It's possibly this; if not, it's likely to be

193

that." He eliminated what it wasn't, explaining how the cold air circulated in this model. If he hadn't had an audience I think he would still have spoken to himself in his head – I know I do. He was quick, deft, confident and thoroughly switched on.

His mobile rang, and it was clearly a workmate in need of guidance. He listened intently, nodding, and then said, "I know. Don't worry; I can talk you through the next stage." What followed was fascinating.

He acted out his instructions in meticulous mime, tucking his phone under his chin when he needed two hands. "Right! Got a table or bench near? Then lift it up and put it on the table. Don't drop it on your foot and be careful how you put it down." He squatted down and placed his arms round the invisible object, denoting clearly how large and heavy it was. He struggled to lift it, staggered to the table and lowered it with commendable control. "Done that? Right! Then rotate it till the circular hole is on the top."

At this point, I didn't register the names of parts and had no idea of the overall plan of action, but I do remember the mime clearly. "Now, pick up the two (can't remember the names) and position them ready to go into the small holes waiting for them but don't try to get them in yet. Done that? They're positioned, and steady? Right! Now, give them a short, sharp *shove* in a slightly upwards direction." As he said *shove*, he gave a thrust that must have put him at risk of a hernia, so convincing was it. He continued, "It should have locked home now. Has it? Good! Do you want me to run through anything else? OK. But if you do, just give me another call."

I said that if I had been at the other end of the call, with the component parts in front of me, I felt sure I could have done the job myself. He said that was the way he had learned, and he had found it worked for others too.

I asked the question I always ask: "How did you come to be doing this job?" Not for the first time, I was told, "I didn't know what to do, so I just got a job and started from there." He told me the jobs he had had and it sounded an awful lot – how come? He said, "Either I get fired or I walk out." I asked why and he said, "I don't suffer fools gladly and often the bosses don't let me do things my own way. Even when I know I am right, I'm still supposed to do what they say."

I said, "Quite right, too!" and he was surprised and asked why. I said I had no problem with jobs done in an unorthodox way – I do it myself frequently – but I don't like arrogance. I wouldn't expect to walk into a new job and start throwing my weight about, and why did he? He said he had never been called arrogant before. I asked, "And are you?" and he said, "Yes."

I asked if there was anyone in the office he would like me to phone to say how pleased I was with the way he had corrected a fault others had failed to find. He said, "Yes – the boss." He gave me the name and phone number and I said I would.

He was halfway down the garden path when he turned and said, "I've just thought of something ..." and proceeded to tell me of a flash of insight he had had – fluently expressed and very much to the point. As he spoke, he waved his hands about and, since I understood that because I do the same, I joined in and gestured with him. He laughed and said, "If ever I lost my hands, I wouldn't be able to talk." Me too!

I went indoors to phone his boss, and the secretary asked if I could tell her the nature of my call. I said Tony had just left and I wanted to say how impressed I had been. She laughed and said, "Well, that makes a change!" and put me through. The boss was splendid, and said, "He's a good lad and very able – I understand him, because I'm dyslexic too." I told him about the master class down the phone and the boss said, "He's very good at that. He has endless patience and can explain things so clearly – it causes quite a bit of friction because some of the older men go to him and that leaves senior staff feeling put out and slighted." He said he would call Tony in when he got back and pass on the message.

I wish I knew where and how the ripples spread out from this series of encounters.

CHAPTER 7

Common sense, intelligence and intellect

Common sense, intelligence and intellect

'Common sense' figured prominently in our everyday language when Pauline and I were growing up – and we always knew that it was highly prized. We also knew that we both had it, which was very satisfactory.

The words were delivered in varying tones of voice in different situations. Father would say in some exasperation, as I had yet another bright idea that was less than bright, "For goodness' sake, use your common sense." Mother used it rather differently. I can see her now, surveying some degree of chaos (from emerging from the dugout after a landmine that fell in the back meadow removed our roof and all the windows, to having to make a decision about choice of curtain material for the kitchen) and saying, "Well, now (thoughtful pause), my common sense tells me that ..."

My own 'cleverness' in that respect was never doubted. I would walk over the fields to Romford on market day when I was about ten, my basket, shopping list and purse full of small change under my full command. Before I set off I used to say, "What do I do if they haven't got this or that?" and the answer was always, "Just use your common sense."

So I did. I noted the alternatives, what they looked like compared with what we usually had and what the various prices were, and made my decision. When I went home to report, I could give all this background information, ending, "So I bought this instead."

Sometimes ignorance let me down (How was I to know that the

biggest lemons were almost bound to have less juice than the smaller, thin-skinned ones?), but no matter what, the reply was always, "Well done! That is exactly what I would have done." This growing confirmation that I had 'common sense' was deeply gratifying and morale boosting.

I don't think I remember the word 'intelligence' being used at all, though in school I came to believe it was something I didn't possess. But so what? I had common sense.

The dictionary defines this as 'sound practical sense, especially in everyday matters', and it was ordinary, everyday living that I so much enjoyed. I enjoyed it so much that having a home, husband and children was the height of my ambition – it would have been my chosen 'career', it truly would. And why should its value be underestimated?

However, I got a training 'to fall back on' and practised it until I had children. Then, for ten years, I stayed at home and brought them up on almost no money at all – and rose to the challenge as a trout to a fly. I branched out to do other things when both children were at school, which led to fulfilling extra dimensions in my life. But I never deviated from knowing that my family mattered more than anything else, and everything fell into place round that.

Slowly I began to understand where 'intelligence' fitted into the scheme of things, and it was a ten-year-old boy at a child guidance clinic who opened my eyes to this. One day I asked him a question, to which he gave the 'wrong' answer. I said, "That doesn't happen to be the right answer, and I'll explain why in a minute, but it was a highly intelligent mistake to make." He looked at me in amazement and said, "I didn't know mistakes could be intelligent." It has bothered me ever since.

I always knew that I had common sense, capability and 'copeability', but it never occurred to me that I was intelligent (that was associated in my mind with good marks in school and exams) until the examiner who tested me for dyslexia told me that I was in fact highly intelligent. By then I was 80 and I wish I had known this before; it would have raised my perception of myself in my own eyes and boosted my confidence.

How are the low achievers – or non-achievers – ever to take heart if no-one ever tells them that they have acted or spoken or coped in an intelligent way?

Intelligence doesn't show itself only in the ability to learn facts that can be given back to teachers in the way that is required and expected. My dictionary defines intelligence as, 'the intellect, the understanding, *quickness of understanding*' (my Italics).

I am slow to learn at the depth and breadth that matters, as I rely on the methodical making of connections in the early stages, but I am very quick indeed when I am open to the forces of intuition.

I can best compare myself to one of Mother's golden Labradors. She had a succession of them, all gentle and intelligent, but the last one, Cora, seemed to be intelligent to an extraordinary degree. When she was quite young, she started having trouble with her right ear. She would be fine for ages, then one day she would go into the farm office, off the kitchen, and take up a position in front of the cupboard where all things veterinary were stored on a high shelf. She would lower herself on her front paws, head resting on the mat, bad ear uppermost, and whine gently. As soon as she was heard, drops were delivered, and she tail-wagged her thanks.

We wouldn't have dreamed of claiming that Cora was an 'intellectual' dog, but it would surely be fair to say she was intelligent. It seems reasonable to suppose that repetition of the relief those drops gave her was stored up until the connection became automatic.

So it is with me, but the important thing from my point of view is timing. If I can make these connections quickly, I am intelligent. But if it takes me ages, am I unintelligent? That isn't how it feels.

One day, when we were gardening, my husband made a comment that caused me to respond with a comparison. He then said, "Do you realise that whenever anybody mentions someone or something, you always say it is 'like' someone or something else?" I hadn't realised, but I recognised the truth of it immediately. In the same way I can think back through these written pages and recall how many times I have referred to the imperative need I have to make connections, knowing that if I don't I will be overwhelmed by the mounting muddle in my head. I can't be hurried over this; it has taken years to build up my connections, and to store them in their separate 'compartments' on the 'shelves' in my mind. For me, this process of organisation always involves first a review of all the relevant experiences involved over the years. Only slowly can I organise them, until the moment of 'grasp' arrives, when I retrieve them in a flash. Children like me need time: to watch, to learn, to sort out and to store.

As 'common sense' and 'intelligence' slowly merged along an imaginary line, so 'intelligence' and 'intellect' merged along an extension of this line. I am grateful to a friend of many years' standing for helping me to visualise this extension. He was talking to me about his two sons, who were "as different as chalk and cheese". He said that one day he and his wife went to an open day at their school and the headmaster came up to them beaming benevolently. He said, "You have two sons, one very clever and one very intelligent. If I dropped them both into the middle of the Sahara desert, it is the intelligent one who would get them home."

The head went on to say that the clever boy would romp through every exam that came his way; the intelligent one would struggle through his exam-taking days but would get where he needed to be in the end if he was interested in what he was doing.

And so it proved to be. The clever one became a doctor with ease – with time to spare for competitive sports and beautiful girls. He is now a consultant orthopaedic surgeon in a large teaching hospital.

The intelligent one had always been interested in anything that grew, flew, wriggled, fluttered, waddled or ran. He also graduated – after a real slog – and then spent four years with Peter Scott at his Wild Life Geese Sanctuary. He said of that period, "He would take me for walks and point out things I would never have noticed, and tell me about them." This rings true for many of us. We learn best by interest-led observation, and from those who can inspire us on the job. He is now working as Diversity Manager for the Oregon Department of Fish and Wild Life, responsible for organising the conservation of endangered species.

Both boys are happily married with children. Both love their jobs and the lives that go with them. Both have 'got there' in their own time and way. Chalk and cheese!

A good upbringing recognises and goes along with these differences – without making comparisons or value judgements, let alone imposing labels.

'Intellect' is a word I never remember hearing at home, but I somehow got the impression that being 'clever' in a practical and intuitive way was as far as ordinary people like us were required to go.

However, the next generation extended our learning on this, as so often in other ways. Two of ours, who went to university, challenged my husband's and my assumptions about cleverness with their own perception that, "We might have been considered clever at school, but when you get to this place and meet people with brains the size of planets, you know you don't even begin!" Even as I write this, I suddenly see that there is also a long connecting line between intelligence and intellect that can extend to genius.

I knew that Mother had been made so unhappy at school, both by the attitudes of teachers (except for one) and by the nature of school work, that she dreaded the same thing happening to us.

And father once told us that his Headmaster had said to him, "Gunary, you have a first class brain but you don't use it – you're lazy," with which father entirely agreed. He was bored stiff at school; having milked the cows before breakfast, he just passed the time as best he could before getting back to milk them again before tea – then it was loading the cart for the Borough Market, or turning the hay, or whatever was required. That was where he wanted to be. That was what he wanted to do – though he did say once that he thought he "might have liked to be a high court judge in India, but not enough to do the necessary work." Even those born in 1885 could have their wannabee moments!

Because of their own experiences, neither of our parents wanted us to be pushed academically if it went 'against the grain' of our natural learning abilities and aptitudes. They had always wanted schools that would be an extension of our family life and values, and that would discover what we were good at and promote it. The older we got, the more difficult this became.

So, when I was 14, they sent us both (with considerable misgivings on many counts) to Sidcot, a Quaker co-educational school in the Mendip Hills, which had a reputation for providing a good general education for children who weren't all academically bright.

I well remember how we arrived, unpacked the car and settled in for the first night, with the assurance that both parents would spend the night in a B&B opposite the school, leaving for home the next morning – with us as well if need be.

The morning came, and we felt unexpectedly happy and confident as we gathered outside the school, together with the

Headmistress, to wave them goodbye. At the last minute, Father it was who had a wobble. He suddenly put his large arm round tiny Dr. Stimpson – clad in the regulation 'headmistress' outfit of navy blue serge costume, a white blouse with a neat brooch at the neck, lisle stockings and sensible shoes, with her dark hair pulled back into a bun at the nape of her neck – and said anxiously, "You won't turn our girls into blue stockings, will you?" She looked up at him, positively twinkling, and said, "We're terrible people, aren't we?" and he blundered on, "*We* think so … ," while she continued to twinkle and Mother just wanted to die of embarrassment in the background.

We took to this whole new environment like ducks to water. We discovered for the first time that it was possible in school to learn and be happy simultaneously. School subjects for me became easier (up to a few O levels, but forget A levels) because of the balancing recognition that I had a hands-on, creative and communicative side to me. For the first time, I felt 'known' and understood at school. Indeed there were so many opportunities and such a very wide curriculum – dancing, singing, art, drama, swimming, athletics and lovely gardens where we could wander – that I was very happy there.

A few weeks ago, I received notification from Sidcot of their campaign for a Creative and Performing Arts Centre. At the same time we were told that the school had recently been accepted to run the first International Baccalaureate course in the Somerset area.

I can testify that 70 years ago the seeds had already been sown, and were growing nicely.

Such schools still exist. Martin, the grandson of one of my colleagues, thrived in one of them. Martin – despite a verbal reasoning IQ of 130 – found it very difficult to read and write due to dyslexia. He had become increasingly unhappy and frustrated after five years of schooling. The family had worked valiantly to help him, but there was anxiety all round that the next school move could tip the balance and overwhelm Martin's confidence and his ability to go on trying to swim against the tide – even though he had exceptional strengths as well as weaknesses. The difficult decision was taken to send him to a school specialising in inclusive education, where 40% – 50% of its pupils have special educational and other needs, and the rest do not. This means that while some children will follow the traditional academic route, there is a broad range of vocational courses, from business studies, art and photography to metalwork, cookery, animal husbandry and horticultural training on the school farm. The pupils are encouraged to market whatever they produce; for instance they sell plants, and some of the products from the woodwork and metalwork departments, to garden centres, and they show the farm animals at local shows. Martin is fascinated by amphibians, fish and insects, and is developing a business rearing and selling stick insects.

Genuine inclusive education at last! What stands out for me is Martin's own progress on every front over the next three years, and his recent summing-up of himself as being "different, because I'm wired up differently".

Me too! I feel like a travelling kettle, which, if plugged into an AC socket, works according to plan – but plug it into a DC socket and it won't function at all.

CHAPTER 8

Coming full circle

Coming full circle

At long last, the learning of the last six years is falling into place. After all the remembering, reflecting, listening and asking questions of almost everyone I met, I am both more knowledgeable and wiser.

I still don't believe there was anything 'wrong' with me during those glorious years of childhood. If I am dyslexic (which I understand is a condition we are born with), then that was the way I *was*, and I enjoyed being an unidentified dyslexic enormously.

If I was already programmed to find reading, spelling, remembering some things, understanding some things and possibly writing and sums difficult once formal education began, then I am even more grateful to our parents for allowing us to enjoy the freedom to play for as long as we could.

We played all day and every day, doing what came naturally. That is what play is all about: self-chosen activity undertaken for its own sake. It isn't what children do, so much as the spirit in which it is done that determines whether or not they are playing. To be asked to set a table is a 'job', which brings its own satisfaction as you feel yourself to be a member of the family team. To set a table secretly, as a surprise, is 'play' with a particularly happy flavour. And just to woozle about, not knowing exactly what you want to do, until an opportunity presents itself, that is another dimension to the wonderful world of play – you enter in, and you opt out, just as the spirit moves you.

By the time we went to school, we could run, hop, skip, jump, climb (trees, walls, fences and in and out of windows), dance, throw, catch, bounce and hit balls, and dogpaddle in the sea if someone walked backwards in front of us. We could also dress and undress, tie shoe laces, and manage a variety of fasteners. We could sort laundry, wash our own socks in the bath with us, and all the dolls' and stuffed animals' clothes in the garden, pegging them out on a low-slung line with hand-made wooden gypsy pegs. We could sew on buttons, make dresses for our dolls and animals, thread elastic through hems and trim our straw hats with flowers, leaves, feathers and anything else that could be held in place with a wide elastic band. We could make pastry (distinctly hard) and toad-in-the-hole (though not the hot oven bit), and scrub and prick potatoes for baking in their jackets. We could also make jellies, sandwiches (if the bread was cut for us) and chocolate crispies.

In the garden there were packets of seeds to sow, pot plants to transfer to our plots, flowers to pick and arrange in vases and jam jars, and cotton-wool 'nests' to fix in the hedges (which the ungrateful birds never used!). On winter days there were Ludo, Snakes and Ladders, Snap, Happy Families, patience, jigsaw puzzles, scrap books and cutting and sticking, using sweet papers, snippings from magazines, and old Christmas cards.

We helped Mother to hang out the washing, handing her socks, underclothes, shirts, dresses – all grouped neatly together. We watched her iron, and did our own hankies when the iron had almost no heat left in it.

Sometimes we liked helping her; sometimes we wanted to do the job on our own. Sometimes we wanted to feel part of the family partnership doing real jobs – but I don't ever remember us wanting Mother to join our imaginative games. We didn't want her to 'pretend' to be anyone or anything, and she wouldn't have dreamed of asking us for a trip on our magic carpet. Mother was Reality. We were free to come and go between reality, copying, pretending, imagining and fantasy. I now think this was particularly important as I watch and listen to young people saying they want to be 'famous' without having had the opportunity in childhood to enjoy both fantasy and reality, and to learn the crucial differences between them.

We were all great carers: Mother looked after us and we passed it on down the line. I cared for my dolls, and Pauline for her Wilf and Ted, on a daily basis, and to us they were real. We moved easily between adult reality and our own child's version of reality – understanding one reinforced our understanding of the other. And sometimes we opted out completely and were just us.

How much more would it have been reasonable to expect of a five-year-old? And there were, and still are, thousands of children like us. Imagine then the shock of going to school, where teachers knew nothing of all this background, and it didn't seem to count for anything. I knew a very small, bright little boy from a lively, happy family, who went into his village school full of confidence. By lunchtime he had got the hang of things. When, after the dinner break, the bell went to signify it was time to stop playing and line up silently in the playground by the door, he summed up the situation at once: the children didn't know what they were supposed to be doing. He went up to the teacher and said, "You go inside and tell them what to do next and I'll stay here and sort this lot out." So she did, and he did. And it worked beautifully. His teacher was delighted and told his mother at the end of the day – and, having got the 'feel' of the family, she continued to treat him as he expected to be treated: as an intelligent person willing and able to co-operate when the situation required extra help. He now felt a member of this new 'family' and he took to learning as a duck to water.

Fairness and equality

But it wasn't like that for everyone. Some of us went in confidently enough, eager for this new experience and wanting to do everything that was required of us – but that was the rub. We didn't understand *how* to do what was required of us; neither could we explain what it was that we couldn't do, let alone why.

There seemed to be a huge gap somewhere. I knew so much that wasn't recognised, or wanted, whilst not being able – for the first time in my life, I think – to switch on to what *was* required.

It is at that point that some of us lose our confidence, and our joy in learning is clouded by anxiety, often leading later to despair.

It is also at that point that guilt and self-blame set in – it seems so ungrateful and unreasonable not to understand. Not only are we different, but we are clearly also 'wrong'. In addition, we are bewildered, because we feel we are being punished for we-know-not-what, while recognising clearly that we are the triggers for what befalls us.

I was never able to bridge this gap, and encountered very few teachers who were intuitively able to bridge it for me – but when I did, it felt like flying.

I had a recurrent nightmare, which ran through my life from schooldays (I think) until my fifties. The only things that changed were two single words; apart from that it was identical every time. Always when it started I could feel myself being drawn into it yet again, but had no power to stop it happening.

I was in a large hall with windows down both sides, but they were so high that only the sky was visible – and it was always grey. I was sitting in the middle of a sea of empty desks and chairs, and on the stage raised above me there was another empty chair and a slightly larger desk with a glass of water on it.

I was alone, more alone than I had ever been in my life. Even the invigilator had left. He had swept past me, clutching an armful of papers, without a single glance. I was so frozen that I couldn't even turn my head to see if the door to the corridor was still open, or if it had been shut on me.

I would look down at the piece of paper in front of me. I had put the date in the top right-hand corner and 'Brenda Gunary' in the top left-hand corner and either *Geography* or *History* in the middle. All were meticulously underlined, with an additional underlining beneath, exactly the same length as the first.

And then, nothing. I couldn't think, or write, or move a muscle. There wasn't a single sound and I couldn't even call out. I continued to sit, and then panic would begin to take hold and I couldn't hold it back – and then, just before it closed over my head, I would wake up.

My heart would be thudding, with fear only just at bay. I didn't dare shut my eyes in case I was drawn back into the nightmare, and I couldn't get up and go downstairs to make tea because there was no energy available. So I would sit on the edge of the bed and wait for the deep distress to pass.

The silly thing is that I passed both History and Geography with a Credit in my O-levels – but what nobody but me knew was that the nightmare was the truth of the matter. I can pass exams (up to a point) without having learned a single thing – except how to pass exams. For me, exam passing was knack, not knowledge. And that came about because I had learned ways of coping with a disability I didn't even know I had.

I thought of this recently when I saw a short item on a TV news programme about the three and a half-year-old who bought an £8000 pink car on Ebay. It caught his eye, he was car mad and had a whole fleet of cars in his 'garage', from miniature size to approximately 10" long. If the monitor screen was smallish, this delectable car wasn't much bigger than his biggest, and – as for the shocking pink colour – who could resist? He knew exactly what he had to do, having presumably watched his parents in action. So he did it. And the first his mother heard about it was when she was phoned and congratulated on making the winning bid.

Luckily, when the circumstances were explained, everyone began to laugh. She was told bids from three-year-olds were not legal and all was well. It was hugely to the child's credit that he knew what he had to do – but also proof that we can reproduce techniques without understanding what we are doing. I did the same with exams all my school life – knowing how to do it but without real knowledge or understanding.

Over the years my feelings of inadequacy about this began to give way to rather guilty feelings of resentment: why *should* I have carried for all these years the scar of failing to pass exams properly? I had tried so hard. So had many of my teachers, but I was the one being 'punished' for something that wasn't my fault.

It simply wasn't fair!

And then something happened, in the way that such things do. One night in August 2006 I went to sleep with the radio still on, and was woken by a woman's voice saying, "This is the six o'clock news." The first item was the GCSE results, just out: more starred 'A's than ever before; better results from girls than boys, but the boys were catching up; fewer people took maths, science and foreign languages; more were taking 'soft' subjects such as art and media studies.

No surprises there – but then, almost as an afterthought, "30,000 failed to pass in any subject." I turned the radio off and just lay there, almost too shocked to think.

I pictured the TV news bulletins to come throughout the day. Cameramen would be in the school halls where the results were pinned on the notice boards – mostly girls' schools, because their over-the-top reactions would be more camera-worthy than the more moderate ones of boys. The girls would be jumping up and down, flinging their arms round one another, hugging, clapping their hands over their mouths and squealing, "Omigawd! Omigawd!" And that is exactly how it was. (On the other hand, why not? They had worked hard and were rightly pleased with themselves.)

But what about the 30,000? Statistically insignificant? Mathematically, yes; morally, no. Each of them is a human being who matters – to themselves and, surely, to the rest of us. We make enough fuss if they become anti-social, and tend just not to notice if they are lacking in general confidence and happiness.

Since these 30,000 are the ones I empathise with so strongly, I leaped to their defence and wanted to shout, "These children have been in full-time education for eleven years, and the system has failed them. And if they are leaving school, not only without a piece of paper, but quite possibly also without the attitudes, abilities and confidence that they need to get a job – then the failure is profound."

What are we going to do about it? Just carry on as before? I could hear some of my friends say, "Now, calm down. The situation is very complex. There are no easy solutions …"

They are right, of course, but I have come too far in these last years to be able to walk away.

I thought back to a time when our grandchildren were at the stage of protesting, "It isn't fair! His/hers is bigger than mine," or "better than mine," or, worst of all (they were just beginning to learn about the cost of things that could be bought with birthday/Christmas present money) "cost more than mine."

We all did our share of trying to explain about cost and value, but such concepts were beyond them in the heat of *their* crisis. So we left it. But when Christmas drew near, their grandfather and I decided we had had enough. We asked then whether they wanted their presents from us to be 'fair' or 'equal'. With one voice, they said, "Equal!" So we said, "Right. In that case, we shall give each of you a football, or each of you a doll. Which shall it be?" And up went the cry, "But that's not *fair!*"

So it is with me again now. I can no longer believe that an 'equal' education system is 'fair' to a whole swathe of children, scattered throughout the country, in every type of school and neighbourhood. What if some of the standard aspirations, goals and teaching methods are not appropriate for all children? What if the national curriculum and teaching methods are at odds with the life-long learning experience and natural potential of many children? What if we are denying them experiences that they urgently need because of current assumptions about what aims are most 'desirable' for them? That really wouldn't be 'fair'!

This is so easy to write, but I can't begin to tell you how long it took me to clarify my thoughts through this veritable minefield of traditional thinking. It couldn't have happened at all if, in these last years of recollections and reflections, I hadn't also asked everyone I met the question, "How did you come to be doing this?" – and if the answer hadn't so often been, "Well, I was never any good at school ..."

It is this that is so unfair, and unreasonable, because so much potential has been overlooked in testing and measuring something else.

Those who gave me that explanation may well have been among the 30,000 GCSE failures of their day – but they were not failures as craftsmen, or carers, or doers of jobs by the time I met them. I just feel sad for all those who leave school feeling they weren't "any good".

Being different

So now, as I recall the long talks with my sister about our childhood, I remember yet again that we both felt that it was perfect for both of us – even though I proved to be dyslexic and she was not.

We were never made to feel we were "no good" at anything, though we were helped to realise that the same was true of other people. We loved the experiences of childhood, and rejoiced in being able to exercise our bodies, our minds and – perhaps above all – our senses, individually and in combination with each other. And in retrospect we were so glad that both parents (in their very different ways) had set the example they did in all the qualities that underpin 'the family'.

We were not 'taught' how to bring up children, look after a home, shop and cook and clean, carry messages, act responsibly, or be truthful – and there were many mistakes along the way. But we absorbed all this by living together under one roof and learning at our own pace and in our own way. Freedom to make mistakes is very liberating – and there aren't many that can't be put right at that age.

I was so ready and eager for school – and it was a shame that I couldn't learn so much of what was taught. The 'me' inside had once felt so strong and capable; where had this person gone?

I can still see no signs of anything other than a blissfully happy childhood. What is more, when I compared notes with my non-dyslexic younger sister Pauline when we were in our sixties, we *both* agreed that we wouldn't have changed a thing about this period of our lives.

Once at school, my 'problem' might have been identified and I might have been given remedial 'help'. Many teachers genuinely want to open doors to experiences they themselves have found rewarding, thinking that if only children could get over the non-reading hurdle the world would begin to open up for them – but my world was already beautifully open. The aim of remedial work would have been to teach me to read and spell so that I could catch up and become part of the main stream instead of feeling 'different'.

But I *am* different! Neither better than, nor not as good as, but different from others in quite a fundamental way, or so I have come to believe. It was *my* difference, not the differences in my reading and spelling, that needed to be recognised and understood.

Anyone who seeks to help others to learn or to understand has to recognise that people of any age can progress only from their own starting point – the level of experience, interest and understanding they have already reached. This is especially true for young children. During their earliest years, they need abundant opportunities to build up a 'platform' of understanding and confidence from which they can safely move on when they are ready to more formal learning. In order to achieve this, they need plenty of time in the beginning for self-motivated play. *All* spontaneous play in early childhood is educational, *so long as it is led by the children and not by us.*

If we try to impose our own ideas about how 'help' can give children a head start, we risk doing more harm than good. For example, there was a snippet towards the end of one of the TV news items not so long ago. The Headmistress of a nursery school said, "We introduce our two and a half-year-olds to computers and they love it. Their parents are delighted too. *We have to remember that children are so much more sophisticated these days."*

No, they are not.

I have heard this said by so many parents and teachers, all of them genuinely concerned to progress children's development, but the dictionary defines 'sophisticated' (of a person) as "cultured and refined; discriminating in taste and judgement". How can a child who has been in the world for only 30 months possibly be any of these things?

Parents will always be delighted when their children appear to be 'getting on', but the fact remains that genuine learning for children of this age starts from where and who the child is, not what we imagine/assume/wish them to be.

When I began working with under-fives in small groups during my Froebel training, I used to picture children being born with their own knitting patterns in their heads – if I stepped back and watched carefully, I could 'see' what kind of a garment was beginning to emerge. It was the child's garment that mattered, not to be diverted or over-ruled by my preferences or addiction to fashion. Tough Arran sweater? Middle-of-the-road jumper or cardigan? Delicate party bolero? It was always individual child development that intrigued me, for only when I began to recognise and understand what was emerging could I sense what the child needed from me.

Although times change, the reality of child development goes far deeper than custom or fashion. These first years are the bedrock of all our lives. If we interfere with children's own sense of timing, as they explore and develop at their own pace, it is the equivalent of aiming to blast off a rocket to the moon when the preparation of the launch pad has been skimped.

The process and the product

I am indebted to so many people – most of whom won't even know how much they helped me to begin to grow in understanding. For years I have been asking people, "How did you come to be doing this?" and found it disturbing that so many of them started by saying, "Well, I was never any good at school ..."

Others said, "I had no trouble doing what was required in school and university – but I suddenly realised I didn't want any of it; it wasn't making me happy."

These people were a revelation to me. Their wide range of abilities, but almost uniform life-style preferences, slowly began to fall into a pattern as I wrote thumb-nail sketches of some of them. Perhaps one day this will be another book – but not now.

I must also thank Julia Race, who volunteered to type what I wrote, and continued to do so literally for years. Everything I sent her was in longhand, mis-spelled and crossed out, and there was a great deal of re-writing at intervals, but she steadfastly found her way through. She was from a business background but managed to come in on my odd wave-length of intentionally erratic punctuation and invented words. When she began to teach IT to adults, she identified some who were dyslexic and found that she first tuned in to them as people, rather than making their mistakes her first target. It has been a mutually rewarding friendship, for which I am grateful.

Then came Ann Henderson. We had worked together with volunteers in the early days of playgroups and were well acquainted with the mixture of gifts and abilities that enabled people to perform at levels that amazed themselves and others. Whether or not they had passed exams was neither here nor there.

Ann reinforced for me what the job of an editor was – to be a go-between, smoothing the path between writer and publisher. Publishers can't take chances, but I couldn't accommodate a change in structure because mine was a fundamental part of my make-up, and Ann understood this. Publishers and editors like prose that flows smoothly from point to point without repetition, but Ann recognised that repetition is an essential part of my learning process.

If publishers were jewellers, they would probably opt for strings of smoothly graded pearls; I can only manage a series of cameos linked together.

Ann can sift and sort material with impressive speed and ease. I can sift and sort, but much more slowly, and when the material is sorted it has to be cross-indexed so that I can quickly retrieve what I need.

Ann's thinking is so clear that she can dart from A to Z quicker than any crow. I can't. I need to go round and round the houses – via the scenic route at that! But when I have mapped it out I know it in great detail, and can retrace it, or dart to any part from any other point, or recall in detail what I have seen and learned.

Ann's clear thinking can eliminate repetition; but she has acknowledged and worked with the fact that my thinking, and that of many of my readers, quite consciously needs repetition. Ann could write a chapter on, say, 'The Discipline of Consequence', covering every aspect, and so clearly that most readers could grasp the ramifications at once. I can't – but at least I know now that it is not because I am unintelligent. I just need to recapture endless different examples of how it worked in a variety of settings – and, as communication is the name of the game for me, I can then select the example that seems most appropriate for the recipient(s).

At the Froebel College we studied the great educators. I couldn't read the books properly, but it didn't seem to matter – I was a farmer's daughter, so of course I understood the importance of nature, and the need to handle wood; to recognise its 'feel' and basic shapes. And it was obvious to me that children and adults who had missed out on any important stages of their lives (such as play, or making relationships) needed to regress in order to make them up.

It was the same with Piaget, and his outline of the pre-requisites before transfer of training could take place. I 'knew' them as soon as I heard them, because I had seen them in action as I watched children. Without that combination of close observation and intuitive understanding, the ability to reproduce the information in a written exam answer doesn't automatically mean that the principles can be applied – especially in the heat of the moment!

In this time of national crisis in education, I remember how much the early playgroup volunteers learned, and applied, without reading or writing or being 'passed' or 'failed'. They learned by working together, every inch of the way, with someone more experienced.

Four old friends from the early playgroup days have shared my thinking as I wrote, and have read chunks of it most willingly and diligently. They were endlessly encouraging – but also asked critical questions and offered suggestions in the most positive way, and for this I was truly grateful. Finally, as the end drew near, I also asked two younger colleagues, from the early days of practitioner-to-tutor experimental courses, if they would bring their critical faculties to bear on something they were seeing for the first time. Their time, thought and astute appraisals were exactly what I wanted and needed.

Almost without exception, I took on board everything the six queried or suggested – not out of tact or courtesy, but because they were right. The six who gave so generously of their time, thought, encouragement and comfort (as in strengthening, not feather-bedding!) were Jean Brown, Mary Bruce, Jill Faux, Sheila Shinman, John Watson and Charlotte Williamson.

At this point, I want to acknowledge help of a different kind. Ten years ago, I fell and broke my thighbone in several places, and it was then that I acquired a team of three remarkable men. They were Kevin Cheah, surgeon specialising in lower limbs, Richard Harrington, selector and adjuster of a long line of soft and hard leg braces, and Len Nugent, a remarkably intuitive osteopath whom I first encountered in my gardening days (and incidentally father of the 'chalk and cheese' sons referred to in Chapter 7).

They were, without exception, the best teachers I ever had – communicating quite naturally in word pictures by way of explanation, exceedingly good at listening, and adept at conveying so much more than was said and done. I felt 'plugged in' to their sockets and everything flowed as I found myself able to contribute fully – no-one ever did their exercises with greater regularity and diligence!

Without fail I looked forward to all my appointments, put on my best 'bib and tucker' and sallied forth to find out how things were going. And without fail there was an informed appraisal, involving questions and answers on both sides, leading to explanations, laughter and a feeling of being boosted and sent on my way rejoicing.

And then, three or four years later, I fell and broke the other leg in exactly the same way – so off we all went again. No denying it was a bit of a blow, but we all gathered ourselves together and everything went swimmingly – literally, as the new hydrotherapy pool was very much a part of all this.

But this time my bones were too old to regenerate, so I am wheelchair bound, but we continue to work together. I am able to go on living alone in my own home, happy and content, with wonderful neighbours – and time to go on thinking.

Not for the first time, my thoughts surprise me. What is it these three men have (and other men and women and occasionally children) that sets them apart? It is more than what they do; it is what they are – plus a particular kind of energy, insight and intuition that enables them to impart this energy to others without even knowing that they do so.

But whatever it is, I am grateful to them, and whether they know it or not, the book wouldn't have been finished without them. Lately it has been tempting to let go, but I promised myself that I would complete it, partly to try to justify the time, skill and friendship that these three gave me.

And now to the unique contribution of Sarah Arben. She came to help me six or seven years ago and we found we were both dyslexic. Although thirty-five years of living separate us, our childhoods and school days replicated each other to an extraordinary degree. The sources of our happiness were the same. Our bafflements, anxieties, dreads and areas of 'failure' at school seemed to have been the same – and so were our cheating, excuse-making and evasions as we tried to avoid being shown up in class. Our reversion to our childhood happiness and confidence whenever we were out of school was a revelation to both of us.

If there was a diploma in home care and management; bringing up children; cooking superbly; creating a garden to gladden the eye throughout the whole year; putting a small sewing machine to excellent use for the home and family; hairdressing; photography and picture making; listening to and caring about family and friends with empathy and understanding; and generally being a lively, loving, responsible and common-sense person – then Sarah would be top of every class.

Sadly, she was always bottom of every class — either remedial or main-stream — because she couldn't read fluently and her spelling, despite being easy to read because of its phonetic accuracy, is admittedly unorthodox.

While I was writing and remembering, Sarah and I have compared notes every inch of the way, so I asked her if she would like to introduce herself to the readers, especially those we hope we may have encouraged by letting them know they are not alone.

She said that she would and this is what she wrote.

Sarah's letter filled almost the whole of a large sheet of lined paper, which provided in its balance and generosity a vivid image of the way she is.

For this reason, we would have liked to reproduce it exactly as she wrote it.

The size and shape of the book prevented this, but the following pages reflect her original as faithfully as we could manage.

I am Sarah I had a Lovely mum
and a good childhood. a happy
Start. I Started School and that
Seemed ok. but I Just couldnot lean
to read. one day I remember siting
on the Sopa in a friends house I cant
remember what we were doing I Just
remember Crying and thinking to
myselph why did god mack me
diferent. everyone else could read
except me. years went by and lack.
of confidence set in. Seconoary Scholl
came. cooking Art nedelwork and Pe
they wennt so bad but mathes and English,
I Just couldnot relat to sqare rods
ect they Just didnot Seem relevant
to anything that I would ever need
in my life and as for french when
I couldnot even master english. I could
add up my monny in my perse and give
change waigh things and mesher
I didnot need all that other stuff
I got a Job in a hairdressers and withun
a year I had Lennt moor than I had
Lennt for years at school. Then came
children I looked at my beutifull
twinboys and I now what I had been made

for everyday was a pleasure. I loved my life having children was just such a fulfilling pleasure. Now I have 3 very different grown ups and am as proud as a mum can be. So what I cant spell but everyone loves getting my letters and im not ashamed of it anymore. I am a mummy and a carer and a lot more besides. I dont want to be a brain sergeon or a solicitor somone else can do that. my friends and family love me just ~~the~~ as I am. Just as I love my friends and family just as they are I feel very lucky. the only regrets is that it has taken most of my life to not feel inferior in some way that I cant read as fast as some. and I do spell dredfully.

Now read again what Sarah has written, focussing this time on what she has to say rather than on the mechanics of presentation.

Would it have helped Sarah to be kept on for yet another year at school? Would it have been any help if pressure – even in the guise of 'help' – had been put on her to learn to spell correctly? Wouldn't an extra year or two, even if this included all the practical skills she was so good at before school, have come too late?

The world is crying out for people like Sarah (and her male counterparts), for her caring skills are in such short supply. She has a huge capacity for learning – but not from books, writing, or being measured by other people's yardsticks. And she has so many skills that were never identified at school.

We have to learn how individual children learn, so that the emphasis changes from teaching subjects to teaching children how to learn in their particular way and to the best of their ability. This will automatically lead to widening the choice of activities on offer in the first years of school so that all children are given the opportunity to shine in their own way.

Recently a friend of long standing, who has shared the experience of writing this book, said something profoundly comforting and I have asked her to write it in her own words. I am content to let her have the last word on my journey of self-discovery. I couldn't have shaped the outcome without her – and she hasn't once put words into my mouth, altered the rhythm of my talking-on-paper, or failed to understand my excessive need for odd punctuation, in order to break up page after page of condensed print that defeats people like me before we even try to read it.

A matter of time

Working with Brenda to help prepare her book for publication, I have become increasingly aware of the extent to which people's view of each other and of themselves is determined simply by history. If Brenda and I had been born before the development of the printing press, I would never have encountered the medium with which I feel most comfortable, and which has enriched the whole of my life. Brenda, on the other hand, would have been valued, as she is now, for her quick intelligence, practical skills and intuitive understanding – and if she had suffered the 'disability' of dyslexia, it wouldn't have presented too much of a problem because it's likely that neither she nor anyone else would have noticed.
Ann Henderson

★★★